Contents

Part Three
Ending Turf Wars

Preface

I once spent three weeks trying to get a copy of our client's year-end sales analysis from a co-worker two doors down. We worked for the same advertising agency, on the same account, and for the same client, so I figured we were on the same team, right?

At first he "couldn't find it." Then it was "probably in Angela's office." But Angela didn't know what I was talking about. Then he was late for a meeting and would "be sure to have it by tomorrow." He didn't. Finally it escalated into a scene (note, I still believed he wanted to give me the report) in front of the elevator. Surrounded by cronies, he started to shine his key chain flashlight up my nose and into my pockets, repeating, "Well, maybe it's in here. Is it in there? Nope. I just can't find those statistics anywhere. Sorry."

As the elevator doors closed, I could hear the laughter echo up through the elevator shaft. Stunned, I stood silently absorbing a lesson that would continue to intrigue me to this day. The fact that it was *his job* to share the sales analysis information with me didn't matter a bit to him. Just because an organization chart said we were on the same team did not make it so. Obviously, we weren't. His actions clarified that issue. In fact, he and I weren't even playing the same game. So there must be two games. If one game was the "Serving the Customer Game," what was the other game? Who made up the teams? What were the rules?

I had heard of this game before. People said, "You've got to know how to play the game," "It's all part of the game," or "It's just a big game."

All I knew then was that I was losing both games. My report was late. I needed the statistics and I didn't have them. Lacking an intuitive grasp of the social game at play (I'm convinced that being an only child retarded my social savvy), I tried to rationally understand the dynamics of this superficially irrational occurrence. Didn't he want to serve the customer? Wasn't his salary tied to our entire team's performance? What was more important to him than money and performance?

As long as I searched for a rational answer, the pieces didn't fit. Only when I realized that my recent success in applying the client's budget to direct mail might mean that some of the TV dollars ("his" area) could get reallocated to direct mail ("my" area) did the scenario begin to fall into place. It was a territorial thing. Obviously, protecting valued territory will take precedence over other group goals (like serving the customer, making money, team success).

He was playing for keeps, too. This was a very serious game. I realized that I could either denounce the game as irrational and shortsighted or learn how to play. I could point out the self-destructive aspects. I could try to "talk some sense into him"—and be eaten alive in the process. Or I could abandon the self-righteous path and learn how to play.

I learned the rules. I learned to make friends in high places, to withhold information, to say I was going to do things I had no intention of doing. I started winning "the game," and I hated it. I thought, and I still think today, that it is stupid to spend so much time and energy jockeying for position, hoarding resources, and manipulating information when we could be spending that time and energy serving our customers.

I don't want to play the game. I want to change it.

Easier said than done, perhaps, but not impossible. My first approach was to delve deeper into the origins of the game. What is the origin of territoriality? Books didn't tell me much, but they got me started. Most of the literature discussed territoriality in terms of physical space, but I knew that the examples I witnessed occurred when people were acting territorial about intangible things. The rest of the literature discussed territoriality in terms of animal behavior and early human evolutionary behavior. I saw some strong correlations and began to believe some sort of biological impulse might be playing a powerful role in our territorial behaviors. I decided that I needed to do more research. You are about to read the results of that research.

I wanted to discover something useful. Not some grand theory, but a useful tool that has enough power to modify a biological impulse. As a behavioral science consultant (I ditched advertising a long time ago), I understand that the wisdom for solutions is more likely to be found out in the field than in some ivory tower full of theorists. People know. They understand what is going on and, when anyone bothers to ask, are willing to share what they know. Everyone I asked about territoriality knew exactly what I was talking about and shared what they knew.

This book is a firsthand report on my research into territoriality. Not lab experiments, but research that taps into the wisdom of these people—the men and women in corporate America who see it and live it every day. It harvests from their stories a behavior-based definition of *what* territoriality is, what it looks like, and exactly *how* it plays out in organizations. To this documented research I have added my own theory for the *why*—that territoriality is an evolutionary-based and perhaps instinctual behavior. I cannot prove it is an instinct, but no one can prove it isn't. Academic debate on this issue may be entertaining but must ultimately end unresolved. For our purposes here, it doesn't matter. If we have to choose a position, then choosing to believe territoriality is an instinct has clear advantages.

Using the hypothesis that territoriality is an instinct gives us permission to see it in ourselves as well as in others (it's only *natural*). We can save a lot of time that way. If it is an instinct, then there is no one to blame, and no value judgments have to be made about what should and shouldn't be. We were born with it, so let's get busy and decide how to manage it. Rather than getting defensive or pointing fingers, we can go straight to the business of changing the behaviors.

In this book, another issue that might divert attention from the business of changing behavior is the academic habit of source citing. Graduate school nearly ruined me. To this day I find it hard to write a sentence without citing at least two or three supporting sources. So let's make a deal. I promise not to quote sources if you'll allow me a brief overview of the many contributors to this subject.

As far as I can tell, the fascination with territoriality began at the turn of the century. A book on bird songs and their territorial purpose got the ball rolling. From that time on, the exploration into the dynamics of territoriality fascinated many scientists. There are contributions from the fields of zoology, ethology, behavioral biology, neurophysiology, neuroendocrinology, sociobiology, ecological anthropology, anthropology, economic sociology, physiological psychology, social psychology, psychobiology, evolutionary psychology, organizational psychology, and so on. Everyone has an opinion. In reading many of these contributions I noted few "No Trespassing" signs, but I still feel somewhat squeamish trudging brazenly into intellectual turf that has been so well staked out. If you are one of those experts in territoriality, please don't shoot. I come in peace.

The theories ranged from seeing territoriality as an instinct to territoriality as a social solution. The instinct school proposes a "let's face it, we're all just greedy animals" approach, whereas the "territoriality is a social solution" school counters with "we are not animals; we simply want to play well with others, and good fences make good neighbors." One guy even apologizes for using the word *territoriality*, saying it isn't a "pretty sounding" word. I fall somewhere in the middle. I think we have instincts. I think territoriality is one of them. But I also hold on to the optimistic view that we don't have to be slaves to our instincts.

The point on which I seem to disagree with all the experts is their insistence that the definition of territory be limited to geographical or physical space. I suspect that this limitation was created more to avoid muddying the field of research than because of a sincere belief that people don't feel territorial about intangible things. (If not, they should talk to some of Microsoft's lawyers about intellectual property.) Therefore, the biggest diversion from documented research you will find in these pages is a broader definition of territory that incorporates information, relationships, and authority.

If you are still interested in background reading, the Bibliography contains an overview of enough books to get you started.

Finally, to those who will say that this book oversimplifies the complex dynamics of an organization, I can only respond: "Yes, it does. And your point is . . . ?" Were I to itemize, define, and explain the relationships between all the factors behind the behaviors described here, I would sacrifice the benefits of a useful theory (not to mention boring you senseless). Allow me to present an oversimplified, inherently inaccurate, and incomplete model of human behavior that almost anyone can understand and use in a matter of hours to change behaviors that need changing. This book is a tool. A tool needs only to be useful to earn its right to exist. Try it out.

How This Book Is Organized

This book is divided into three parts. The first part gives an overview of territoriality as an evolutionary adaptation. It discusses the emotions involved and my redefinition of the territory worth protecting in today's organization.

In the second part, a chapter is devoted to each of the ten territorial games. At the end of each chapter is a brief self-test that will enable you to explore your own experiences for signs of territorial game playing. If you want to skip ahead and go straight to the games, that section starts in Chapter 4.

The third part presents some practical recommendations for dealing with territoriality in your organization. You will find individual exercises and descriptions of several group processes that you can use to decrease dysfunctional territoriality in your organization.

How the Research Was Conducted

This book is based on in-depth research I conducted in a variety of client organizations and which was enhanced by the privileges afforded by long-term client/consultant relationships.

Based on the use of qualitative methods, the research included more than forty in-depth interviews. Interviews were conducted with middle to senior-level managers of moderate-size (100 or fewer employees) to large (1,000-plus employees) organizations. For obvious reasons, these organizations prefer not to be named here.

Each interview was approximately one hour in length. Interviews were nondirective and open-ended. The interviewer extracted the interviewee's definition of territoriality with probing language such as, "Tell me about a turf war in your organization," and used continued probes to extract a functional definition: "Tell me of an instance in which you witnessed what you would describe as dysfunctional territoriality. What did the players do? Who initiated it? How did you know? What behaviors communicated that message?"

All interviews were recorded and transcribed to a written verbatim format. The resulting 200 pages were analyzed for recurring behavior patterns. Eleven unique patterns emerged from the data. These were labeled and defined. The verbatim manuscript was then refined into 143 intact anecdotes that were categorized into the appropriate pattern categories. One of the categories was dropped because it occurred exclusively in only one organization. The ten remaining categories are presented here.

Acknowledgments

Thanks to the wonderful people who told me their stories. As promised, in the book they remain anonymous, but I remember them and am most grateful.

The support of my friends and family was vital to the completion of this book. I want to thank specifically Cheryl De Ciantis and Sherry Decker for never-ending words of encouragement and David Williams for taking care of the household repairs so that I could write. Thanks to Ken Matthews, who tested the material in its early stages. Thanks also to Jim Farr, my mentor, whose support and encouragement spurred me on when times were tough. And thanks to Quinn Dalton, whose diplomatic words of guidance helped me to bring order out of chaos.

I dedicate this work to my grandmother, Olive Burt Simmons, who taught me to stand tall, look 'em straight in the eye, and call it like I see it.

Part One
Understanding the Impulse Behind Territorial Behavior

1

Genius Into Gruel

"A turf-conscious manager [can] grind genius into gruel."
—Thomas A. Stewart, *Fortune* magazine

That's the problem, isn't it? Creative spirits, motivated enthusiasts, and innovative drivers become the casualties of an organizational turf war. Once people start wrangling for a territorial advantage, pushing their hidden agendas, and undercutting their peers, no one is focused on organizational goals. The turf war mentality lowers our sights, and we waste valuable time and effort crushing an enemy who could be, and should be, on our side. We lose too many valuable resources to the "friendly fire" of organizational turf wars.

And it's getting worse. In our effort to do "more with less," we have inadvertently inflamed new turf wars as people fight for more of the "less" they are supposed to be doing "more" with. Now what?

When fights over limited resources and rewards siphon off the valuable creative juices of a work group or sabotage organizational goals, we usually have one standard response: We sit in someone's office or gather over a beer and we gripe about it. The clichés and jargon peppering our language is testament to the frequency of these gripe sessions. We call them turf wars, power struggles, office politics, and ego battles. We identify factions, camps, and empire builders and malign their destructive influence on our ability to get the job done. And then we shake our heads and shrug our shoulders as if the whole pattern were an unavoidable fact of life. Some of us hone our political skills with the philosophy that "it's a jungle out there" and that it's "do unto others before they do unto you." Others take the peacemaker role. Very few try to understand the wars well enough to end them.

This book is a tool for those of you who are tired of fighting the wars and tired of playing the games. Einstein said you can't solve a problem with the same thinking that created the problem. So we need a new way to look at turf wars. My goal is to reframe the discussion of turf wars and territorial games so you can stop looping through the same old solutions and conversations that bring you right back to where you started, with nothing changed.

A New Perspective: Studying the Opposite of Cooperation

Everyone is so focused on increasing cross-functional cooperation, collaborative efforts, and partnering arrangements that they don't stop to focus on the forces working to prevent cooperation. When people aren't cooperating, what are they doing instead?

I have counseled many executives who said they wanted to learn to listen better. My standard approach is to tell them, "Find out what you are doing instead of listening and stop doing it." They think I'm crazy at first. But eventually they admit that they are usually trying to get to another meeting, talking on the phone, or thinking about what they are going to say next. One client described his definition of listening as "the time I have to wait before I get to talk again." At least he was honest. These executives didn't need listening skills. They had been to "listening skills" courses. They knew all about "active listening." They could nod at the right times, hold eye contact, and even "reflect back" a paraphrase of the speaker's words. They had the "skills," but they still weren't listening. They didn't need to learn how to listen. They needed to learn how to not "not listen." We don't need to learn how to cooperate. We already know how. We went to the training session. What we need is to learn how to not "not cooperate." And more important, what drives us to not cooperate.

There is a broad base of knowledge out there concerned with creating good ways to cooperate. Management consultants, training professionals, human behavior experts, and others have contributed theories, processes, and strategies to increase the forces for cooperation. Powerful group processes designed to increase cooperation are readily available. So with all those forces helping work groups to achieve cooperative behavior, how can we explain the uncooperative, apathetic, and divisive behaviors that we see? What is the force driving some people to withhold information? Is it to exclude an entire department from the strategic planning process? Is there some hidden force working against all our well-intended efforts that generates uncooperative behavior?

Cooperative Behaviors >|< Uncooperative Behaviors

Forces for Cooperation ----->|<----- Forces Against Cooperation

Vision

Values

Team building

Etc.

?

This book holds that there is a hidden force in all of us that limits our desire to give 100 percent wholesale cooperation. We have an innate desire to hold something back for ourselves or for our group (however we define that). This hidden force could be labeled with any of a dozen labels. In order to study and discuss it we have to choose one. I have chosen to label the force driving uncooperative behaviors a *territorial impulse*.

Studying the Territorial Impulse

More than a definition, we need a blueprint describing the observable characteristics of territorial behaviors *in organizations*. It isn't important to understand the territorial behaviors of animals or the territorial behaviors of den mothers at a Boy Scout meeting. We don't need to understand the territorial behavior of the three-spined stickle-back fish—although their territorial dance of snorting bubbles at each other and then aggressively shoving their snouts in the sand and staring each other down has its corporate correlates. No, in order to define territorial behavior we need a blueprint. We need a list of specific behaviors (I call them games) that precisely define the territorial behaviors occurring in corporations today, as described by eyewitnesses.

Just as we might film the stickle-back fish, why not observe the real McCoys and Hatfields in their natural habitat, and study their habits? Imagine video cameras positioned in your conference room and hidden in the halls and photocopy room—and the documentary that could be created about behaviors at product design meetings, budget meetings, team-scheduling meetings, or hallway discussions of work in progress. This book is like a written documentary of those behaviors.

Interviews describing the behaviors in today's organizations that represent the opposite of cooperation were collected like miles and miles of film. This book is the edited version, grouping like with like, drawing conclusions, and offering ideas on the origins of these behaviors.

After analyzing hours and hours of interviews with people like yourself, I have developed a list of the ten most common and most destructive behaviors displayed during a corporate turf war. For simplicity's sake I call them territorial games and devote a chapter to each, beginning in Part Two. However, I feel it is important first to consider the *why* of territorial games before we look at the *what*.

Playing Territorial Games to "Survive"

The territorial impulse is deeply rooted in our survival programming. We are territorial because territory helps us survive. It did so thousands of years ago and it still does today. If you look at it backwards, survival needs started the whole concept of territory. The problem now may be that we are still using old territorial behaviors that are no longer appropriate to our new environment.

Defining "Survive"

It used to be so simple. Survival opportunities were food, sex, shelter, and good hunting grounds. Survival threats were lions, tigers, bears, natural disasters, and anyone else who wanted our food, sex, shelter, or hunting grounds. Necessary emotions included fear, anger, and desire. Our prehistoric shortlist of behaviors included things like fighting, fleeing, grabbing more, having sex, and marking borders.

Life is actually simpler today in terms of survival issues. We don't have any, at least not real ones. Certainly not in corporate life. Who was the last manager you knew who died from a loss in market share? Who was executed when she ran over budget? It doesn't happen. Yet we use words like *killed, injured, flesh wound, invade, defend.* We talk and act as if our survival were on the line.

The truth is, our egos are on the line. In the unfortunate logic of neuro-association, self-image got mixed in with the survival programming. The emotional equipment designed to protect us from lions, tigers, and bears and to help us find food, sex, and shelter keeps running even when the lions are in cages and our tummies are full. We are being run by out-of-date programming that operated for thousands of years to perpetuate the survival of the species. Our threat response system (the limbic system—more on that in Chapter 2) remains, hanging around waiting for an emergency so that it can take over our more rational brain and propel us into a repertoire of defenses and attacks designed many, many years ago to protect us. It reminds me of Barney Fife waiting to jump into action. Barney got tired of waiting for real emergencies so he got creative. Just like our limbic system.

No real threats? We'll create some. No unmet physical needs? Fine, let's find new needs. Here is where it gets interesting to hypothesize. What are the basic human needs? Abraham Maslow's hierarchy of needs is as good a guess as any. He says humans begin with needs of hunger and thirst and, once those are satisfied, move on up to security and protection, belonging and love, self-esteem, and, finally, self-actualization. Just because our culture may be climbing up this ladder of needs doesn't mean that there has been a correlate redesign of our biology. We have the same limbic system for self-esteem needs that we had for hunger and thirst needs.

When self-esteem is threatened, it is as if our psychological survival has been threatened. When we see opportunities to enhance our self-image, it can stimulate desire as strong as that felt by a caveman looking at a ten-dinner-size prey. The limbic system snaps into action, generating emotions like fear, anger, and desire. Each emotion prompts some preprogrammed impulse to act, and we mindlessly allow these impulses to drive our behavior.

Territory and Survival Needs

At some point we humans developed an awareness of past and future. When considering needs this is a very important concept. Territory is the answer to meeting future needs. Without territory we have to start over every day to find new ways to meet our needs. However, if we can appropriate a little land to call our own and protect that land, when we wake up tomorrow morning our shelter needs are handled. If we were smart enough to find some prime real estate, then our hunger and thirst needs require much less effort as well.

As evolution progressed, our limbic system—always scanning for a survival edge—picked up on this fact. "Find and protect territory" had to have been one of the first impulses for the primitive human as he scrolled through his crude list of things to do today. From this perspective, we can view territoriality as a primitive instinct, right up there with the urge to reproduce.

It is important to see that the urge to occupy and own territory does not automatically label us as aggressive. Many theorists jump straight from the conclusion that man is a territorial animal to the conclusion that man is an aggressive animal. While we have done our fair share of conclusion jumping, this one is problematic. It is a jump from what we want—territory—to how we get it—through aggression.

The *how* of territoriality is much more diverse than that—just look at the different territorial games. Aggression is only

one of our territorial behavior options. Building alliances is another. Taking the position that humans are aggressive limits our
view. If forced to choose, I prefer to think of humans as innately
greedy rather than mean. I believe we have the option to override this basic instinct. But we are biologically programmed "to
want," to be greedy—for power, influence, and self-esteem, for
whatever we think we need to improve our chances for survival
in the corporate environment.

Territory and Self-Esteem Needs

I hope overuse of the term *self-esteem* has not resulted in your
wholesale rejection of it. All of us have a picture of what we need
to "make it in this world." Think of your corporate self-esteem
criteria. Think about what you "need" to be. Do you need to be
powerful, rich, smart, always right?

One of your self-esteem needs probably includes the need
to see yourself as not having many self-esteem needs. Your mind
tells you that only insecure people have trouble with self-esteem.
That's bull. Everyone has a hidden list of "must bes" and "must
haves." What earns you the right to keep your job? Was it that
last report you prepared, the success of the product you
launched, your reputation as a troubleshooter, the thoroughness
of your records, or perhaps your humility? What symbolizes
survival prospects to you?

More important, what actions would you take to protect
your "survival" prospects? Consider your reaction if another executive were brought in to write your monthly report for you.
What if "your" product were allocated to someone else? What if
someone else started to shoot trouble better than you do? How
would you feel if the MIS people allowed companywide access
to all your business files? Play with any of these scenarios and
you will very likely find an invisible boundary that identifies
the personal territory you hold as a guarantee to your corporate
survival.

Your survival mind/limbic system knows exactly where the
boundaries lie. For one manager, knowing that everyone thinks
his division is growing and profitable is as satisfying as biting
into a big piece of buffalo and knowing that there's more out
there is to a caveman. For someone else, being a vice president

by the time she is forty, driving a Jaguar, or having access to financial reports in advance represents personal territory worth protecting.

The criteria of self-esteem become an unconscious score-board against which individuals measure themselves to determine their psychological survival prospects. And it is the prospect of tomorrow that worries us most, creating a strong motivating force on our behavior. The desire to be a success in our own eyes gets us out of bed in the morning, fuels overtime, wakes us up at night . . . and prompts us to play territorial games like staking out territory, sending out twenty-five copies of a CYA e-mail, and hanging on to information just a little too long.

Territoriality: Nature or Nurture?

At the beginning of the century, theorists on the subject of territoriality started with birds—and how bird songs serve the biological function of marking out territory. You can find an animal to prove just about any theory about territoriality you want. Take our cousins, the primates. Some monkeys are downright friendly while others, like the howling monkey, are very territorial. Howling monkeys routinely scream bloody murder as a group, every morning and every night, to notify neighbors of their position. Unexpected encounters with their neighbors (they are rather nearsighted) get resolved by impromptu screaming matches until presumably each group retires to safe ground to nurse aching eardrums and jangled nerves. (Don't let it be lost on you that this is the sort of thing that happens when you leave it to evolution to choose your survival behaviors for you.) Even gorillas vary widely in their tendencies to be territorial: Some are and some aren't.

Since our purpose here is specific—to identify and change counterproductive territorial behaviors in organizations—we don't need an *ironclad* theory. We need a *useful* theory. Just to cover all the bases, let's build an argument for two theories: territoriality as instinct, and territoriality as a result of cultural programming.

Territoriality as an Instinct

Even if many of the behaviors you categorize as territorial don't seem rational, territoriality makes sense when you think about it as a survival instinct. You see, instincts aren't directed through the rational mind. That's why we call them instincts. We needed a word to describe the things we do when we don't think first. Instincts are primitive and survival-based. They are preprogrammed into our behavior like the migratory paths of the brown trout and the Canada goose.

Since "instincts" don't occur as a result of rational thinking, we frequently label them as *irrational.* Actually, we call them irrational only when they don't work out too well. When our "irrational" impulse works out just fine, or earns us a promotion, then we refer to it as *intuition.* Only the screwups earn the label of "irrational." Yet these impulses (good or bad) might come from the likely source of our instincts, the limbic system. The limbic system is the part of the brain that can override rational thinking if it deems the situation a survival issue.

Instinct, Impulses, and Emotions

We depend on behavior that is impulse-driven. From extreme situations like lunging to save a child in the path of an automobile, all the way to mindlessly driving an automobile, we act without thinking. Our mind is *designed* to create action without thinking. Thinking takes too much time. Edward de Bono, in *I Am Right, You Are Wrong,* proposed that if our mind processed all available options, it would take us two days to get dressed in the morning and a week to decide what to eat for breakfast. Instead, our mind operates on automatic, doing basically the same thing over and over again until a threat or an opportunity pops up. Survival threats and opportunities activate the limbic system and emotions, which activate automatic programs pre-written for immediate application. Thinking is usually saved for when we have lots of time.

Survival-based instincts cause us to react automatically to protect what we feel is valuable and to grab more of what we see as valuable, if we can. If this is too abstract, why not try your own little experiment? Go to a co-worker's desk (preferably someone who is not overly fond of you) and start picking up items from his desk and putting them into a brown paper bag. Observe carefully the facial expressions of your co-worker. Facial expressions are the best reference point for reading emotions. If he does not yet register emotion, try to simulate an invasion of territory by standing nose to nose with this person. Now, evaluate the emotion he is experiencing and note the automatic program that emotion seems to activate. Note how the individual does not seem to call upon his rational mind as he punches you in the nose; it is as if he is reacting *instinctively.*

You may not want to try this experiment too often, but it can provide you with useful data about emotion, instincts, and territoriality of the physical sort. A more detailed discussion of emotion is presented in Chapter 2.

Since we don't have enough information to say conclusively that territoriality is an instinct, let's look at it through the lens of social conditioning.

Territoriality as an Evolution of Culture

Exploring territorial behaviors as socially learned reactions helps us see the role that groups serve in acquiring and protecting territory. This group aspect is important to understanding territorial behaviors in organizations.

The clichés "united we stand, divided we fall" and "all for one, one for all" refer to the survival function of groups in our evolutionary history. There are certain advantages to being in a group. Cooperating by sharing resources is more efficient than trying to survive alone. If we weren't born knowing this (i.e., did not have this instinct), then very early on there was an innovative caveperson who figured this out and taught everyone else.

Group Survival, Group Territory

This behavioral tendency to group ourselves and to throw all our resources together into one shared territory has contributed to our survival as a species. As with successful physical characteristics (like the opposing thumb improvement), behavior has evolved and continues to do so. Some behaviors no doubt became extinct through natural selection. Behaviors like poking everyone you meet in the eye were probably short-lived. Other behaviors, say washing food, were rewarded for their survival benefits.

At some point, we must have developed the urge to group ourselves into collectives, sharing the responsibilities for food gathering, constructing shelters, protecting the babies. Those collectives initially focused on two major issues: safety and food. Wandering groups were bound to notice that some places were safer and had more food than others. In fact, there was probably one place that, for them, was the safest and offered the best food supply of all. Because there was food and shelter they didn't need to stray too far away, and over a period of time they kept falling asleep in the same general area. For whatever reason, the group decided to hang around. The place came to be regarded as "theirs."

Eventually, their focus moved from today to tomorrow. They discovered that with planning, tomorrow could be easier than today. All they needed to do was to store a little extra food and keep it safe. Possessiveness evolved as a behavior strategy to meet future needs. Hoarding food and shelter was rewarded by the evolutionary selection process. Sharing everything with everyone wasn't.

Mine, Yours, and Ours

Hungry bands of protohominids finding a roots-and-berries-full, saber-toothed-tiger-free version of utopia liked their utopia and stayed there. Then it began to feel like home (the word *home* is the very essence of territoriality). Strange cavemen and women wandering into it were asked to leave. The caveperson equivalent of "this mine—you go find your own" was probably delivered at varying levels of enthusiasm ranging from a grunt to jumping up and down yelling and screaming. Scaring others with displays of aggression worked, too. Behaviors that worked were repeated and taught to the young.

Some bright member of the group discovered that marking the boundaries saved a lot of time and energy. If the markers were scary enough (skulls on sticks probably worked well) or flamboyant enough, then wandering invaders would back off without so much as a growl. No fights, no screaming—very efficient. This was a big discovery. It was no less important to the survival of the species than the invention of metal tools or the wheel. Marking boundaries greatly improved the reliable supply of food and water. It was another behavior that made the evolutionary cut.

Kin relationships were the criteria for group selection. The size of the group was very important. It could never become so large that the members outstripped the food supply. Even larger groups would subdivide themselves into more manageable units. There were limits.

Sharing within the group served the purpose of being a group in the first place. Sharing outside the group was not encouraged. Children had to be taught who was in- and who was out-group. Members of the group developed a thousand subtle and not-so-subtle indicators to keep everyone clear on membership. Eye contact, body language, identification markings, even identifying habits could clearly communicate an invader in a second. Once an invader was spotted, the entire group could spring into action to expel the invader. No strategies were discussed. The group didn't sit around talking about how each individual felt. They just called upon their stored social rules for response to an invader and acted. The group developed a bunch of prepackaged automatic responses that accelerated response time to threats and thus survival prospects. These prepackaged automatic responses became a part of the culture. They still are. They constitute the origins of the territorial games we play today.

Survival Training for the Organization

How much of your social training can be traced to territorial programming? You learned that valuable things are either yours, mine, ours, or theirs. Much of our social fabric can be traced to the acquisition, marking, and protection of valuable property. Entire occupations are devoted to the issue of possession. Lawyers, for instance. Natural selection probably favored groups that carved out "more than enough" territory over groups that were happy to get by with "just enough" (whatever that means). So, in survival terms, everyone has probably learned that a certain level of greediness is good.

So if everything valuable ends up as someone's territory, and we are preprogrammed to want more than we really need, how does that translate to today's corporate environment? First you need to consider the concept of value. What is valuable to us today? Back in prehistoric days *valuable* was probably limited to food, shelter, sex partners, and the patch of ground they occupied. *Valuable* was directly linked to the things that helped us survive and thrive.

Corporate survival is a much more complex issue. We may not face life-or-death situations, but we still want to "survive." Whatever helps you survive is of value to you and will inevitably be tied to territorial preprogramming. Whether it is a budget allocation, control over a project, or access to the best and the brightest staff, that which is valuable to you will generate a territorial urge.

A New Environment

Whether through instinct or a deeply ingrained cultural habit, territorial strategies are played out in the corporate drama. We are marching to the ceaseless beat of a drive to acquire and protect what we need or think we need. Farther and farther removed from any evidence that confirms or denies the value of our efforts, we seek substitute measures.

Physical evidence of success, like the big office, isn't as relevant in cubicle-land. The evidence we use to confirm our value and to ensure our survival has evolved to reflect the information age. In the agrarian age, owning land gave us that warm cozy feeling. In the industrial age, money and equipment moved our attention a step away from land. In the information age, the increase in complexity has shifted our attention even farther away. In order to survive and to feel valuable in the information age you need information—to have access to it, to know a friend who does, or to have authority over someone who has information.

Fewer and fewer study the science of farming corn and wheat, because our survival now depends on our skills in farming information. Groups form to plant information, harvest new information, and process it for market. To a large extent, farming information means planting and tending relationships. Good relationships can ensure a good crop of information. Bad relationships at the very least require more energy to produce the same return. Survival now demands the psychological skills of self-management and relationship management.

Corporate survival requires psychological survival. And threats to our psychological survival are everywhere. As organizations continue to reorganize we need someone to tell our limbic systems that everything is going to be OK. Because up to now survival depended on knowing where you belonged and what belonged to you. No one knows anymore. Ego needs easily met through the trappings of titles, perks, and clear lines of authority are now left to find other sources of satisfaction. A preoccupation with psychological survival has replaced physical survival as the underlying force motivating much of our behavior at work.

Psychological survival always reflects our internal criteria for a successful self-image. What happens when we come up short or someone else thinks we've come up short? When our psychological survival is in danger, all rational thought ceases and the limbic system steps in with an "I'll handle this" attitude. Fight and flight strategies translate to arguing, defensiveness, or worse. A simple wrong answer to a CEO can result in a cover-up that makes Watergate look reasonable. Survival programming takes over our brain and we go "territorial"—but over what?

A New Definition of Territory

What is the psychological equivalent of food and shelter? Resources, rewards, budgets, compensation, perks, and status are the loot involved in corporate territorial battles. If that is what you win, what are the pieces on the game board? Information, relationships, and decision-making authority.

To access resources, you need information and you need to be liked by the right people. Or simply have the power to decide who gets what (or who hears what, who sees what). It's the same for rewards. Try to think of a territorial battle that couldn't be won using information, relationships, or decision-making power.

Consider this example: The implementation of a new sales tracking system at Apex Company would seem to be a straightforward affair. Straightforward except that the design of the new tracking system was not submitted by Gary, the current manager of the sales department. Gary's design was rejected in favor of the one designed by the "new guy," Mitchell, ex-sales manager of the Valley Company, which had recently been merged into Apex. Mitchell's design was superior for a variety of reasons, and everyone agreed it would improve organizational productivity.

Therefore, Gary was ecstatic about implementing the new system, right? (See, you know this stuff already.) No; if it succeeded, it would constitute a direct hit to his ego. So with his psychological survival in danger, Gary used information, relationships, and decision-making power to win this turf war.

He probably called it the "new *Valley* System" and rolled his eyes every time it was mentioned. He professed to be "very open to new ideas," and would be "behind it 100 percent, *if I think it can work*. But you've got to understand that [insert some rational-sounding criticism here]." He held private conversations with his salespeople about how he was "genuinely worried" about the new system. He joked with the MIS staff about going slow, "since it will probably disappear anyway." He set up limited training time in a noisy environment and ran informational meetings at 6:30 A.M. Through the manipulation of information, relationships, and decision-making authority, he created his desired outcome: failure.

The Currency of Information, Relationships, and Authority

There are three kinds of territory in the corporate survival game. The first and most valuable is information. Information is power. All the way from the latest marketing statistics to knowing who skipped the company picnic (and why they skipped it), information is the currency that will ensure our survival. Information is often more valuable than tangible goods. Which would you rather own—a new computer or the patent for its design?

The words *intellectual capital* indicate the spiraling market value of information. As it becomes more and more valuable, information is treated just like anything else of value. It is hoarded, protected, even stolen. Following the primitive drives in our nature, we operate as if the one with the most information wins.

Likewise, there are two other corporate "territories" that are so powerful in gaining access to information that they are coveted by anyone focused on winning the corporate game. Relationships and authority constitute direct access to information. Controlling or influencing the control of information is almost as good as owning it.

Relationships, as corporate territory, are relentlessly pursued through the practice of networking. Instinctively, corporate players dedicate large amounts of time to the establishment, development, and protection of "contacts." "I have lots of contacts in that area" is tantamount to saying "I have power." You have seen people with questionable competence hired for their contacts. Good relationships with important people are valuable territories worth protecting. Not everyone actively constructs a "network" of contacts, but all successful corporate staff develop and nurture important relationships.

Less clear as formal authority diminishes, but of great value to our survival prospects, is the authority to make decisions. Authority is, by definition, power. Authority is the ability to make budget decisions, initiate research or a new project, and also to kill a new project. Authority has a direct link to self-esteem needs and psychological survival. Jockeying for positions of authority is nothing new. There are just new rules. New organizational structures and their reliance on informal authority leave this valuable territory up for grabs. The battles waged today are no less passionate for their lack of clarity. They are simply fought with new weapons technology. The manner in which authority is won today depends more on image and interpersonal relationships and thus is more susceptible to territorial tangling. The present unregulated negotiations for authority have evolved into wheeling and dealing of a kind more appropriate to the black market.

Vying for information, relationships, or authority is the objective of a territorial game. And half the time that we are playing these games, we are so focused on our ego's definition of survival that we are screwing up the very organization on which we depend. In Chapter 2 we will explore the internal dynamics that operate to compel us to wrangle for information, relationships, or formal authority in ways that can contradict our own best interests.

2

Why Smart People Play Stupid Games

"All of the eagles and other predatory creatures that adorn our coats of arms seem to me the apt technological representations of our true nature."

—C. G. Jung

Territorial impulses can strip rational human beings of their ability to make good decisions. Below, a familiar battle between production engineers and safety staff demonstrates how stupid (and dangerous) these games can be. The production engineers, focused on speed, productivity, and output, wanted to keep the procedure guys out of their hair because they slowed things down.

> "So there would be cases where people wanted to get something done and regardless of any of the procedures or who was accountable, they would just get it done—they'd go ahead and do it. They would ignore the procedures and then justify it on the basis of this is what you've got to do to be good operators and keep the plant on line. . . . They do that only to pay a great price in the long run because if the design change wasn't done well or wasn't done right—sooner or later you'd pay the price of it not working or the plant shutting down. To keep the procedure people out of their hair,

they were secretive in many cases. In some cases, they would rewrite procedures on their own and not get a technical review."

So? What if you knew that this is a nuclear physicist speaking and that the plant in question is a nuclear power plant? The idea that successful territorial games are keeping the safety procedure guys out of the hair of the nuclear power plant guys is crazy. But situations like this happen every day in many organizations. They may not endanger the survival of thousands of people, but they could be endangering the survival of the organization.

A Map of Enemy Lines

We all have a map inside our head that identifies allies, enemies, and the corresponding territorial lines. Most mental maps are too small, like the one suggested above. Production people viewed the procedure guys as the enemy and acted accordingly. If they had considered the bigger picture of nuclear plant safety they might have changed their map. Risk would have become the enemy and they would have behaved differently.

Without regular "big picture" experiences that build big maps, our maps shrink to represent our daily experiences. Your "survival mind" uses your day-to-day conflicts and meaningful friendships to construct its map of friends and foes. When you think first and then act you probably operate with your "big picture" map. But when you act without thinking (which is most of the time) your survival mind uses its smaller map to identify allies and enemies.

Sound like psychobabble? Here is a symbolic picture of the kind of map I mean.

Figure 1 is a re-creation of a map drawn by ten cross-functional members of a software company. These people had been brought together "to improve the flow of information across the company." Everyone had an opinion. The MIS guy wanted to buy more hardware. The software engineers complained of too much information and wanted more staff to handle it. The production people wanted access to a design engineer for torture

Figure 1. One Group's Metaphor Map of Its Corporate Terrain

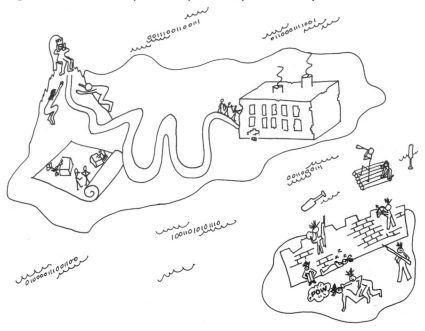

and interrogation at the beginning of each week. The meeting was going nowhere.

Finally, I asked them to draw a map of their organization. I asked them to use their imagination and draw in metaphors, using whatever symbols they needed to communicate the current situation. That map told a story.

It showed the CEO high on a mountain with bowing yes-men (and women) telling him what he wanted to hear. The factory was on the same island as the mountain and connected to the main office by a narrow, winding, treacherous-looking path. The denizens of the main office were referred to as carpet people by factory staff. Since this company was in the South, the term *carpet people* may have referred as much to legendarily exploitative carpetbaggers as to the carpeted main office.

The design engineering staff barricaded itself behind a wall in a fiercely protected fort far away on a separate island. Both islands were placed in a "sea of information." The design engineers were armed with weapons to protect them from incoming attacks related to meeting deadlines. Behind the fort walls, fist fights frequently erupted among the unruly knights. Several were defiantly inactive—sitting, lying down, or waiting.

A lone raft, without paddles or a rudder, was making its futile way to the main island carrying the production engineer and a human resources peacemaker, who were attempting to forge cooperative alliances across the watery divide. The factory off to the side of the map looked remarkably like slave quarters. There were obvious racial overtones. No one in the main office staff was black. The only black person of the ten was from the factory.

Most of these individuals were shocked by some aspect of this map. Unfortunately, the discussion came too late to do much good, as the company was too far gone. Territorial divisions had been allowed to develop to the point where relationships had deteriorated. Distrust was the rule rather than the exception. Apathy and blame were diverting creative energy from solutions. In response to the lagging productivity, the corporation that owned this once-creative company implemented major layoffs. No word yet on the result of this action. The dust has yet to settle, but there are early indications that the holding company is now perceived as the enemy.

Using Their Map to Make Sense of the Games

It is almost as if our survival mind demands a battleground. You can argue this until you are blue in the face, but go ask anyone in your organization or any other organization to draw a map of territorial lines within the organization. Not only can they do it without blinking, but they will invariably demonize one group and idolize another. With a map like that, the games make sense. You gotta survive, right?

Consider the experience of many average employees today. Their bosses have implemented a new organizational structure designed to encourage everyone to share resources and work across old lines of division. They have probably been reengineered, downsized, or reorganized. Their new organizational structure looks fuzzy next to the clarity of the old hierarchy.

New organizational designs like the matrix design now have employees answering to more than one boss (I've seen up to five). This is meant to integrate equally important but frequently competing priorities. For instance, answering to an engineering boss as well as to a marketing boss will theoretically cause staff to better weigh the cost of a new design against the sales benefit it adds to the product. Tough decisions are distributed to the people who best understand the issues. From a rational standpoint, it makes sense. But to the survival mind, people are now put in the position of serving two masters. Shifting the conflict of interest doesn't resolve the conflict. It just shifts it, and in the process creates a no-man's-land of confused loyalties.

For a real show, visit an organization with a matrix structure of five reporting relationships for one person in the first week after the reorganization. You will see a flurry of proposals, e-mails, and meetings that resemble kids scrambling for candy after the piñata bursts.

In these environments, people respond to the disruption with an impulse to find or build a safe place among the remains. Some busy themselves gathering up the spoils of the carnage; others hunker down. But everyone takes some action to secure a bit of territory that will ensure their "survival." They are reasonably sure the organization isn't going to take care of them, so it is every man and woman for him- or herself. And if that means playing a few games, so be it.

Of Course, They'll Deny It

Most territorial games are played beneath the surface. No one can argue against cooperation. Who is going to stand up and say, "Excuse me, I personally enjoy infighting because it meets an irrational need I have to occupy and defend territory, so pardon me if I sabotage your project"? I don't think so. We deny any such need. We deny it to others and we deny it to ourselves.

Denying an internal need doesn't mean that the need stops driving behavior. It just means that the individual is no longer aware that the need is driving behavior. We make up other reasons for doing what we do. One manager I interviewed described his vehement defense of a territorially inspired decision when even he could see that it was a stupid decision. When somebody challenged it, he jumped to the defensive, made up some cock-and-bull reason, and dug his heels in even deeper. As we talked, he laughed at how silly it was. He could see that he was being territorial. He could see his bald-faced denial for what it was. But he didn't go back and change it. He just shoved that distasteful bit of self-awareness right back into unawareness. When we get caught doing something territorial, we deny it.

People always have a rational excuse for their behavior. The psychologists call it "excuse-making behavior" or the "legitimization of choices." When you are the one doing it, you probably call it "a very good reason." When others are doing it, you call it "bull." Either way, after-the-fact explanations only cloud your ability to understand the games.

The truth is, people rarely stop to think and consciously choose their behaviors. That is why smart people play stupid games. They just act, and when they don't know why, they make something up—because understanding territorial games means admitting to irrational behavior.

Understanding and Accepting "Irrational Behavior"

If you want to understand territorial games, you have to accept the fact that the behaviors you observe do not reflect rational behavior. In the sense that the behavior is emotionally generated and operates from the survival and not the thinking mind, it is irrational.

Unfortunately, people seem to think that a behavior labeled irrational deserves no further investigation. The act of labeling it as irrational means to them that it can't be understood. Or that it should be ignored. Irrational behavior *can* be understood. It only requires that you understand the map being used and the "survival" issues that surface on that particular map.

Ignoring irrational behavior leaves you wide open to suffering its effects. Many of the new models of organizational structure seem to have been developed for humans who behave rationally. I don't know where they are going to find these humans. Maybe the designers buy in to the image of the rational, conscientious, self-sacrificing, workaholic most of us portray at job interview time. But, as long as we have to work with the irrational, insecure, and easily distracted humans you and I know and love, we need to spend some time looking at the irrational side of their behavior.

Emotion as the "Jerk" of Knee-Jerk Games

Most games start with a knee-jerk reaction. The force behind a knee-jerk reaction is emotion. In the book, *Emotional Intelligence,* Daniel Goleman points out that the word *emotion* is derived from the Greek words for *to* and *motion. Emotion* means "to move," not "to think and *then* move," just "to move."

If most of our actions are generated without a conscious choice to move, what drives them? Experts generally cite the limbic system as the point of origin for emotion. Up to now I've referred to the limbic system as the survival mind. It is time to hypothesize a little more about the limbic system. Since we have already agreed to engage in gross oversimplifications of highly complex issues, let's not stop with the limbic system.

Basically, it is a storehouse of learning and memory dedicated to the recording of past and the recognition of future events that present survival threats and opportunities. Its filing system is so good that just about anything remotely resembling a past threat (threats seem to get priority loading) is immediately recognized. Once a situation is deemed a survival issue, energy pumps through the body in the form of emotion activating a predetermined shortlist of action programs. The limbic system doesn't take time to bother the rational brain until action is already under way. It simply overrides the rational brain.

> *"I guess we all have been guilty of displaying territoriality. I guess it most often occurs when you're presented with changes to the way that you historically operate. Sometimes it happens without even realizing it."*

People play territorial games "without even realizing it." Once a territorial war has begun, the survival mind often thinks the battle is for real. Those individuals whose psychological survival is totally wrapped up in the territory of intangibles like information, relationships, and authority are the ones who escalate territorial games. One manager interviewed warned of "not being able to separate yourself from your responsibility." When that happens the survival mind has full command of your behavior control panel.

A young product manager, emotionally distraught at having "lost" part of "his" budget to another department, forgot that it was not "his" money. Stalking out of a room, plotting his revenge, and snubbing his peer in the hallway were indications that his limbic system/survival mind had kicked in and emotion was driving behavior. The behavior that is appropriate when someone takes $200,000 of *your* money is very different from the behavior that is appropriate when a decision is made to shift $200,000 of the organization's money from your product to a peer's product. But once in the grip of territorial emotions, he acted as if his "survival" were at stake. As one seasoned executive put it,

"When the boundary has to do with who you are, then you're a goner."

The Emotions of Territoriality

What does it mean to be a goner? The term *goner* refers to an individual whose rational, objective thinking skills have left him. The rational person we usually see and interact with is gone. In his place is an emotionally driven robot. In some sense, he is no longer in control but at the mercy of his emotions.

Remember, emotions were originally designed by evolution to jump in and take over when we needed to pursue or protect our survival. If we were threatened or came upon a survival opportunity, a burst of just the right chemicals directed our bodies to react. But long after we evolved a rational neocortex, the emotional brain still has the power to override the slower neocortex in any survival situation. At their best, emotions help us survive. At their worst, they turn you into a goner and a game player.

Looking through the narrow lens of territorial impulse, we can label three primary emotions that drive territorial behavior: fear, anger, and desire.

Fear

With issues of territorial impulses, the core emotion behind territorial games is often fear. Any level of self-awareness requires an intimate understanding of the anatomy of fear. Being blind to your fear is to risk being run by it. It is of such critical importance in our survival that fear has evolved a special prominence in the functioning of the brain. Because of this, the brain seems designed to tolerate a much higher error ratio of unnecessary fear rather than to allow the possibility of leaving the body defenseless. We are wired to overreact in preference to underreacting.

Fear narrows the focus and heightens the reactivity of the brain. It stimulates physical changes in the body, increasing heart rate and raising blood pressure. It floods the body with instructions, slowing breathing and freezing some muscles. Fear primes the brain to look more carefully for threats, perhaps even to see them when they are not truly there.

Fear is the basis for a variety of feelings. We call these feelings apprehension, suspicion, concern, anxiety, wariness, caution, and so on. Corporate behavior driven by any of these forms of fear is likely to result in a territorial game. A vague apprehension is enough to cause someone to hold on to vital information just a bit too long or maneuver a key agenda item to the bottom of an overly long list. It doesn't have to be full-blown paranoia; a nagging concern is enough.

Anger

Anger is another primary emotion driving territorial games. Anger is the emotional response that occurs when you can't get what you want or think you need. The emotion is hard to identify because people rarely call it anger. Instead, they use the business words for anger, like frustration, resentment, exasperation, annoyance, indignation, and, in extreme cases (usually behind closed doors), outrage or hate. As I work with groups in developing self-awareness, one of the more amusing rationalizations I hear is, "I was angry, but I didn't let them see it." Give me a break. When you are angry, it seeps from every pore of your body. It distorts the face and contracts the vocal chords.

Trust me on this: If you are angry, they know it. Most people would do well to stop trying to hide their anger and look at what it is doing to their behavior.

Anger prompts a wide array of behaviors in organizations. Anger can be "in your face" or "behind your back." Whenever personal territory or psychological survival (read self-esteem needs) are threatened, the limbic system is likely to jump to the rescue with an instantaneous dose of anger. If fear puts the body on yellow alert, anger creates a full-fledged red alert, torpedoes at the ready. Anger further increases heart rate and floods the body with enough adrenaline to fight *and win*. If fear shifts the mind's focus to see a threat, anger seems to shift the focus to see weaknesses susceptible to attack. Mindless attacks can result. The focus of the attack just as mindlessly defends or counterattacks, and a minor conflict spirals into territorial warfare. A sarcastic sidebar or a disparaging remark about "tables that never add up" can stimulate just enough annoyance to begin the escalation.

Desire

Run an experiment with me here. Think about something you would like to have or control in your organization. Stare off into space and think about how it would be if you could get exactly what you wanted. If you keep thinking about it until you have a smile on your face, you have created the emotion called desire. Other desires include hunger and sexual desire. I assume you are familiar with those. Desire, like fear and anger, comes from the biological wiring concerned with survival. (Anyone who studies neuropsychology is, by now, probably appalled at these gross oversimplifications. Sorry. This is my attempt at Emotions 101.)

Desire moves you to take action to acquire and protect anything you perceive as valuable or necessary for your psychological survival. Desire can propel people onto the bandwagon of a successful project, activate their brownnoser behaviors, or cause them to sit silently as a peer hangs herself in excess rope. Less is known about the physiological changes associated with desire, but research indicates that desire affects judgment, especially when the issue is already fuzzy. If you desire it to be true, it is much, much easier to believe that it is true.

Therefore desire not only drives the impulse to acquire territory but can also influence an individual's perception of reality. People only hear what they want to hear and only see what they want to see. Desire for valuable territory drives people to draw maps that glorify "us," demonize "them," and justify their territorial games.

The Rules and Patterns of Emotion

When co-workers (or committee members, or neighbors, or your spouse) become embroiled in a dispute that has "become emotional," the rules of logic no longer apply. The emotional system and systems of logic operate in different paradigms. Emotionally generated actions are not available for rational analysis. Requiring a rational explanation for an emotional behavior is the same as asking someone to lie to you. They have no choice but to make up a rational-sounding explanation. Demanding a "rational explanation for their behavior" only takes us farther and farther away from understanding the root-cause drivers behind the uncooperative behaviors troubling organizations today.

Incorporating an understanding of emotions and emotional intelligence into our organizational designs and processes requires an open forum. Organizations that have been unwilling to look at the emotional nature of employees will find many of their fundamental assumptions challenged. To recognize and openly discuss fear, anger, and desire and the irrational patterns they drive means learning the rules and patterns of emotion. To make this easier, I have categorized the worst of these irrational patterns as "games."

Territorial Games

In organizational life, when someone pursues a hidden agenda, says one thing and means another, or otherwise subverts the common good for his or her own undisclosed ends, that person earns the label of being "game-y." This language evolved to help us articulate the kind of behavior that really gets our goat. When we say someone is playing a game, we are usually saying that he or she wants to win, at someone else's (our) expense. Territorial games and tactics focus on winning ownership of coveted turf. Even if the turf in question is as intangible as being the company expert on a particular subject, the game is the same.

Calling these behavior patterns games allows us to separate the behaviors that are destructive from those that are functional. In Chapter 3, I discuss how being territorial can sometimes be good, but playing a territorial *game* means allowing emotional impulses to drive behavior past the point of the common good. The term *game* was first used in this sense by the transactional analysis people. It is such a useful concept that I have borrowed it, and offer a new definition of a territorial game.

> TERRITORIAL GAME: a behavior pattern, driven by the need to secure or protect valued territory, that:
>
> 1. Is usually not obvious to the game player
> 2. Is not ultimately in the organization's or the game player's best interest
> 3. Causes bad feelings and stimulates more games in others

You may believe down to the tips of your toes that the individuals playing territorial games "know exactly what they are doing," but it is highly unlikely that they are aware of the full extent of their own behavior. They honest-to-god *believe* that someone else started it, that they have been forced into a corner, or that they are just doing their job. One of the primary forces holding these counterproductive behaviors in place is a complete lack of awareness. Everyone is aware of everyone else's territorial game, but no one sees his or her own.

If you agree that most people would not continue to engage in behavior that was destructive to the organization (and ultimately detrimental to themselves) and you also agree that there is as much territorial behavior going on as this research indicates, you can draw only one conclusion: People don't know they are doing it. Just as the Apex sales manager who killed his rival's new tracking system was unlikely to admit that he was feeling threatened, most territorial defenders are truly under the impression that they are behaving rationally and in the best interests of the company. That is why territoriality is so tricky to describe.

We deny it exists particularly when we are the ones engaging in it. Sure, "we know it when we see it"; the problem is that we only know it when we see it *in others.* Not only do we have a natural tendency to deny our own participation in turf wars, but because today's valuable territories involve intangible turf, the games are harder to spot. It is hard to get a handle on it because "it" is invisible. Try not to use "its" invisibility as an excuse to stay blind.

Games have a self-perpetuating effect because they are habits. Steven Covey has done a fine job articulating the good habits of highly effective people, but we need to understand our bad habits better. These bad habits are deeply ingrained because they evolved from survival impulses. They used to be good habits that helped us protect turf. Now the world has changed and we need to, too.

Choosing which bad habits to drop is tricky. It takes two (at least) to play a game, and once the games are on they create bad feelings and more games in response. That makes going cold turkey a risky business. What if all those jerks really *are* out to take your turf? You might just end up stripped bare of title and budget, left out of the information loop, or even jobless. Or you might end up increasing sales, cutting design time in half, and getting a promotion. In the end, that is the best way to identify a stupid game. Stop playing it, and if things get better, it really was a stupid game.

Getting a Kick Out of Playing Games

Human behavior is full of paradoxes. People smoke even though they know it is bad for them. They jump out of planes for the adrenaline buzz. We only hurt the ones we love. And so on. This realm of human behavior is no different.

For some people the prime motivator behind territorial games is to have fun. They enjoy the intellectual stimulation of a real live game of King of the Mountain. They play it with the enthusiasm with which kids approach a new video game. You can almost hear the sound effects—"POW!" "WHAM!" "Oh-h-h, Bet that hurt"—as they smirk their way through meetings at which they have the upper hand, think of more and more clever ways to keep information from another department, and giggle at the brilliance of a particularly effective put-down. It was no secret to the people I interviewed that some corporate games were played for fun.

"Turf wars are fun. People love it. They get a buzz out of it."

Some even admitted to enjoying a bit of territorial play themselves.

"It is fun to go ahead and stake it out and fight rather than having to be objective. It's easier, more fun. It's fun to watch people do that. I'm envious when I see someone just say, 'Well, I don't give a damn. That's the way it is.'"

Whether it is true or not, there is a perception that men get a bigger kick out of it than women do. They may just be more open in their winning celebrations.

"There's something about men—that is probably that they're more likely to kick into the battle mode, to draw the limit, enjoy the fight, just for the fun of it."

The fact that territorial game playing can be fun makes it all the more difficult to control. When a behavior is culturally reinforced, rooted in survival instincts, emotionally generated, and *fun* to boot, changing it is going to be difficult. There will have to be some very, very good reasons.

3

The Line of Diminishing Returns

"The coward regards himself as cautious; the miser, as thrifty."

—Publilius Syrus, *Maxims*

Being territorial has helped us survive. It still does. Just as our fight and flight instincts are useful, so is some level of territoriality. After all, we really *do* need to survive psychologically. And without us striving to meet our own expectations, our organizations wouldn't get very far. The territorial impulse motivates creative effort and supplies checks and balances to help distribute resources and rewards. The need to identify with a group territory aids us in clarifying roles and responsibilities. It helps us get along. Good fences make good neighbors, and well-staked-out territories prevent duplication of effort and wasteful renegotiations on who does the dirty work.

Many organizations simulate old territorial rituals and symbols to encourage this "good" territoriality. We mark ourselves with company shirts and hats. At group meetings we blow up graphs and charts of our competitor's successes to enhance the perception of external threat ("they're gaining on us") and to tighten the ties that bind us to each other. We reinforce perceptions of what is "rightfully ours" or of what we want to be "ours."

Territorial behavior can just as accurately be described as competitive behavior. Competition provides a valuable source of energy for corporate success.

Telling the Difference Between Good and Bad Territoriality

Where does competition end and territorial games begin? There is no clear distinction between the two. The only way to tell is to carefully consider which people matter most to you and to evaluate the ultimate impact on them. Your frame of reference completely determines your definition of good or bad territoriality. The territoriality that prompted the bombing of Hiroshima was either good or bad depending on your nationality, background, and basic values. Territoriality that protects the research and development budget for next year is good if, on your map, you are on R&D's "side," and may be bad if you look at the company as a whole. The transfer of health insurance from the public to the private sector will be good or bad depending on your beliefs about the role of government and which people are important to you.

When the R&D department is strongly territorial about a new product and protects its brilliant designs from a "pessimistic" engineering department, is it good or bad? It depends. If you are the one who will be laid off if they cut the budget it is bad, unless you are also a stockholder. And even if you are a stockholder, it isn't clear; they could either waste a lot of money on designs that never work or take the market with a groundbreaking innovation.

It is impossible to develop an objective definition of good and bad territoriality. It depends on a subjective value judgment. That's like having an opinion on whether spitting is good or bad. It really depends on what you have in your mouth, who is around, and where you are. If you are having tea with the queen, you might want to resist the impulse regardless of how much you hate cucumber sandwiches. If you just bit into a poison apple, it's probably a good idea to spit. In the end you've got to decide for yourself. It's the same with territoriality. Sometimes it is good and sometimes it is bad. It just depends.

The Law of Diminishing Returns

When territorial lines accurately match the organization's boundaries, things work very well. It is when an organization has an internal civil war—an "empire builder" in its midst—or when internally drawn lines of territoriality operate to subvert the organizational good that territoriality becomes a problem.

Fuzzy as the concept is, there seems to be a consensus on the point at which we are reaching a diminishing return in organizations today. When asked about territoriality, people seem to have a common wisdom about bad territoriality and the destructiveness of the games played in organizational turf wars. And people know it when they see it.

Recognizing dysfunctional territoriality will never be a science. You can't apply rational analysis to an irrational behavior without missing something. The best you can do is check in with enough people to make your map big enough to see if you or your group has crossed over the line of diminishing returns.

A good rule of thumb is this: If a bigger-picture view of your territorial behavior indicates that you are damaging your own best interests, your map is too small. If you are the center of your universe or if your work group is, then your map is too small. You may find that some of your territorial games translate into "cutting off your nose to spite your face." And if you think this is not about you, think again. There is no harm in drawing a bigger map just to make sure you are not crossing the line into diminishing returns.

Crossing the Line

A certain amount of territoriality is inevitable. The people I interviewed expected it, particularly where there were geographical distinctions. It caused a problem only when the territorial players crossed the line and became "defensive and parochial" or labeled relationships as "mine" and "you can't have it."

> *"Where I've encountered it most is in the manufacturing and the plant arena. Our manufacturing people are very territorial—maybe it's because you can draw a physical boundary around that territory. It is a plant. They are incredibly defensive and parochial."*

> *"There is the logic versus the politics of the territories. Some of the territory stuff is maybe somewhat legitimate in that*

*you have a customer relationship and they like to stay in one
location. I don't think that is substantial. What is more of a
game is this—something having always been my territory
and feeling you can't have it."*

Human beings have a need to categorize things, people, and
events into manageable pigeonholes. It reduces the complexity
of the world. In organizations, customers get allocated to certain
territories (usually geographical) and tasks are grouped into departmental or functional responsibilities. For the most part, this
works. Until limited resources cause the fences separating functions to get so high that cooperation is prevented.

Organizations have often used internal competition as a
prime source of motivation, particularly with sales staff. The
general attitude was "let 'em duke it out." Sales incentives pitted
salespeople against each other in an effort to tap into that ol'
competitive spirit—which is fine as long as they aren't withholding information, fudging figures, and stealing customers from
each other.

*"They [subdepartments] tend to compete with each other
more than with our competitors, which is not what we had
in mind."*

*"We had an organization before . . . that almost promoted
territorial thinking. It was territorial in the sense of geogra-
phy. We measure all of our performance on a regional profit
center basis. In terms of the way the budget was developed,
within those regional profit centers they competed against
each other."*

This competition is so deeply ingrained in our culture that
we become blind to the point where we have crossed the line and
are playing destructive territorial games instead of indulging in
a bit of healthy competition. We forget the bigger picture and all
we want to do is win the battle.

*"It's a belief that in order to win you have to beat someone
else. I'm bottom-line-driven to a quarterly reporting process.
An old theory that comes out of high-strung college and ath-*

*letic experience, which is what most executives associate
with: Competition is good, competition is healthy. That just
breeds infighting. When you pit one division against another
division, you're creating a turf war."*

The trick is to identify when the competition crosses the line
and becomes an internal turf war that can sabotage the organization's goals. It operates by the law of diminishing returns. The
goal is to maintain the delicate balance between what is good
for you and what is too much.

Tragedy of the Commons

In discussing the point of diminishing returns for territoriality,
it is useful to look at sociological research into the ways humans
have traditionally resolved the issue of diminishing returns. It is
not good news, folks.

Someone even made up a name to describe what happens
when wants and desires escalate to the point where people act
against their own best interests. It is an old term that indicates
we are talking about an old problem. It comes from the observation that when using a common grazing area, farmers will inevitably escalate the size of their herds to the point where the
common area is overgrazed. Rather than limit their personal
gain and maximize the benefits of all, they almost always overdo
it to the point where everyone loses. This phenomenon is referred to as the "tragedy of the commons." In direct contradiction to the "rational" alternative of survival for all, most of the
time we humans mindlessly obey our internal urges to want
more. Historically, our rational minds are overruled by impulses
and emotions that compel us to always want just a little more—
even if we will pay for it dearly in the end.

Of course, you can't eliminate the importance of the "if they
do it, then I will too" syndrome from our choices to overgraze,
grab, hoard, and so forth. One of the more interesting methods
of researching these phenomena has been the "prisoner's dilemma" paradigm—an artificially created situation in which
two individuals are asked to pretend that they are being interro-
gated separately for a crime they committed together. It is

explained to them that if they both keep quiet both will get a short sentence. If one rats on his partner, that guy's punishment will be reduced to a suspended sentence. But if they both rat, both will be prosecuted to the full extent of the law. What do you think they do? Yep, most rat on each other and they both lose.

Is this our nature? To overuse resources until there are no more? To sell each other out for our own self-interest? Research shows that it is—unless . . . unless we first talk it over. In the prisoner's dilemma research, improved communication between the two increased the likelihood of a cooperative decision. Group dialogue and outside facilitation have been shown to increase cooperation in similar games. (More advice based on this research is presented in Part Three.) So even if the territorial impulse is in our nature, we don't have to cross the line.

Only if the territorial impulse is left undiscussed (beneath our awareness) will it operate independently of our rational thinking and counter to our bigger-picture survival prospects. It doesn't have to be a tragedy if only we understand it well enough to do something about it. Part of understanding where we cross the line means understanding the situations in which we tend to act territorially.

Us and Them

How do you know who is "us" and who is "them"? Up to now, we have focused primarily on the functional distinctions in organizations. Other lines of territorial division occur between professional groups. The accountants tend to stick together. The engineering staff, marketing staff, or sales staff can become territorial. It is unclear whether this cohesiveness is due to a shared perspective or the bonding effects of frequent interaction. Both, probably. Time spent together also plays an important part in the development of territorial groups. Time together develops ties that bind. Lines can occur along family ties (nepotism) or because of them (sibling rivalries).

There are other familiar territorial lines that operate in organizations—like the lines between different genders and races. Men and women act as if they are in competition for limited territory. Race leads to all sorts of in-group, out-group behaviors. After living overseas, one of the more distressing experiences upon my return was sitting down near a group of a different race and hearing the conversation die and feeling tensions rise. I had forgotten the "rules" of racial division and they reminded me that I was not on "their" side. We haven't made enough progress in erasing this territorial boundary.

The popularity of "diversity" training indicates the prevalence of these kinds of territorial lines. Organizations know that discrimination against co-workers based on gender and race sabotages group performance. And racial discrimination isn't present only in the home office. As organizations become truly global, discrimination disrupts cooperation between cultural factions. Derogatory names like Kraut, Jap, Slant-eye, and Euro-weenie don't do much for cross-cultural cooperation. An expected battle between marketing and production can equal World War III when each department is in a different country. Territorial battles that incorporate the issues of race or gender can get emotional very quickly.

In addition to the important ethical issues driving the diversity movement, race- or gender-related territorial battles have obvious bottom-line implications. Discrimination can impede the flow of information, subvert good decision making, and replace enthusiasm with apathy.

Discrimination is just another aspect of territoriality. The games are the same whether territory is being protected from women by men, from blacks by whites, from whites by blacks, or from unions by management. Some of the better diversity training programs incorporate emotions into the territorial discussion, but few pinpoint the specific behaviors that create the experience of discrimination. Saying "we will stop discrimination" is difficult when no one can articulate or categorize the behaviors that divide. The chapters in Part Two address this need. The description of "shunning," or pointedly ignoring a person's presence or contribution, is a territorial game that women and minorities know only too well. Now we have a name for it. Very few individuals will continue to engage in an activity that is truly counterproductive to the success of an organization that is necessary to their psychological (and physical) survival—*once they see it.*

"Seeing" Territorial Behavior

Most people's self-images do not include the greedy, territorial, hoarding behaviors of which they are sometimes capable. Sure, some people enjoy turf battles and fight them with full awareness, but even these individuals are unlikely to continue fighting a turf war if the spotlight turns on them. The problem for understanding, or even seeing, territorial games is that no one enjoys this sort of spotlight. That is why these games are cloaked in secrecy. Through unspoken "I won't call you on your games if you don't call me on mine" agreements we keep this stuff under wraps. So, in order to see it you will need to look for it.

In Part Two, we deal with the ten most frequently reported territorial games used to defend or acquire territory in an organization. Awareness alone operates as a powerful influence on behavior change. If this book works, you will see your own behavior in the game descriptions and in the future you will notice more often when you are being territorial. You will think more about the implications and effects of hoarding information, relationships, or decision-making authority. Once you are more aware, then you can consciously choose whether you want to be territorial or not. You may be doing it when it doesn't serve either you or your organization.

Removing the Blinders

There are beliefs that will operate as blinders if you aren't careful. For instance, if you are attached to the belief that nothing will ever change, stop reading now because you are wasting your time. More specifically, I have found that there are two assumptions about why people play territorial games that will prevent you from learning anything from this research:

1. People are being intentionally vindictive when they play games.
2. If they aren't being vindictive, then they are stupid.

Since we don't have a cure for vindictiveness or stupidity, you can stop now if you think these are the causes of territorial games. On the other hand, if you are fed up with the games to the point where you are willing to try a new approach, why not entertain the notion that most people are simply unaware of the implications of their behavior? If you can read the following pages from that position, you will see many more possible solutions than if you are convinced that these games are only played by people who are either mean or dumb.

We must overcome old assumptions about territory and break through the hidden nature of these territorial games. As a start, let's look at the games that are being played.

Part Two
Ten Territorial Games

4

The Occupation Game

Possession is nine-tenths of the law.

One of the most basic territorial strategies human beings use is the strategy of *occupation,* that is, maintaining a physical presence on the territory or taking visible possession of the turf item. The occupation strategy works on the physical level because two bodies cannot occupy the same space at the same time. At the intangible level, it means people can't hold two mutually exclusive perceptions of ownership at the same time. The territorial player who gets there first or who is most visible creates the primary perception of ownership. Using the game of occupation, an individual or group can "own" a project, a product line, a department, even a process or methodology, and benefit from the status and rights of that ownership.

At the physical level, imagine a game of musical chairs. When the music stops, either you get to the chair first or you win the butt struggle and knock the other person off the chair before he or she knocks you off. In the end, the winner is the one who is physically occupying the chair. Using the strategy of occupation at the intangible level is a lot like musical chairs. The three "territories" of information, relationships, and authority can be held like a chair carried around by a player unwilling to allow anyone else access. Or a territorial player can simply stay seated during the music. The "occupation" players have already claimed their territory while other less territorial employees are still waiting obediently for the music to stop.

Initially, it is easier to see occupation operating at the tangible level, but a closer look will reveal the intangible level of the occupation game. Marking the perimeters is of principal importance. A well-marked territory is easy to protect. Better yet, owning all the roads in or out of the territory will ensure sovereignty. In the case of information, this means operating as the sole channel for valuable information; in the case of relationships, monopolizing the valued individual's time; in the case of authority, preempting all other decisions with a widely publicized or previously implemented decision. Occupation is all about controlling access by being there first.

Staking Out the Territory

You can easily spot occupation at work when it applies to physical territory or possessions. Three supervisors, in allocating space in a steelyard, played the occupation game until senior managers couldn't find a place to park their cars. In this yard, there were three different types of steel stored in each of three different corners and supervised by three different supervisors. Over time, as new deliveries spread farther and farther into the middle of the triangle, they overflowed into the parking lot as each supervisor commanded more and more space for his "territory":

> *"We had three different departments on the same physical site. When a load of scrap was in, you sent a truck and you had to dump it somewhere on the ground. It seemed to me that the guys were doing whatever they could to sort of define their boundaries and dump piles of stuff in a place that would keep the other guy from using the space. If you needed the space and you needed to take some square footage from another guy, you really had to go to work and explain why you needed the space. . . . There would be this stuff sort of creeping into the parking lot.*
>
> *"The other funny thing is that the people who did the work couldn't stand to get the pile too low. It scared the hell out of them. It was like they liked seeing this big pile of work right there; they always knew they had a job coming. Con-*

trary to the financial side, the best thing we could do was to have no inventory with no money tied up in it."

Tots in a sandbox or adults in a steelyard? It is easy to visualize these three supervisors maneuvering big trucks and building thirty-foot-high piles of steel in a giant version of King of the Yard, panic sweeping over the supervisor who was temporarily out of markers (steel inventory) to defend his hard-won territory. The decisions these supervisors were making on a day-to-day basis served their personal territorial needs more than the needs of the company. Many of their day-to-day decisions involved the strategy of occupation to identify and defend "their" territory.

Think about where you see, firsthand, the strategy of occupation in your own organization (or in your own behavior). Occupation is usually accompanied by the telltale pleasure of having "more" to be kept "safe" from others. Occupation is staking out ownership over valuable property by being there first and by being there in a way that prevents others from occupying the same space. Occupation is about laying claim. Consider the professor who would

"put his name all over everything. He would label everything like rooms. He was never direct or confrontational. . . . He had more subtle ways of doing it. He wouldn't say directly that he wanted something but he would go out and get it by claiming it."

Wolves urinate on the perimeters of their territory. Humans also use symbolic markers to stake out territory. Intangible territory must be marked with intangible markers. Intangible markers exist only in the mind. Marking lines of occupation therefore requires mental markers. The name of a project can mark it as territory. Volumes of memos on a particular subject can appropriate a project to a certain territory. Speaking up frequently as the "champion" of an initiative can establish a line of ownership. Strategically designed personal, one-on-one conversations that influence critical individuals' perceptions of ownership are yet another means of marking perceptual boundaries in the minds of other organizational players. Good boundaries help establish roles and responsibilities, but at the game level occupation markers can create a misallocation of resources.

Shortage of Resources or "Sandbagging"?

When meeting rooms are shared by different departments, the strategy of occupation operates at a very physical level in a series of preemptive moves. The department with responsibility for administering the sign-up sheet, or the person with the room key, usually controls the room. In the following case, this control turns into an occupation game as one department appropriates the room for its exclusive use, thus leaving the resource underutilized.

> *"I've seen a fight over turf as control of meeting space. A rule around here is that we can use any conference room as long as you clear it with whomever is doing the scheduling. . . . That has become a territory issue where a manager will say 'don't give the room to those people even if we don't have anything going on.' We may need to have a meeting and we'll have no place to go. I don't want to be caught without having a place for a meeting if I need one. Even though the system is set up so that we all share, I will 'sandbag' my meeting room."*

"Sandbagging" a room, good people, computer access, or financial resources (by spending the money before anyone else can) means allocating resources on the basis of a group's territorial skills rather than on the basis of optimizing the organization's needs. The occupation strategy allows a group or individual to stockpile resources while other groups or individuals are left in need. The result is equivalent to a bona fide resource shortage.

> *"I know that a lot of times they hide some of their better people—the qualities of their better people. . . . So while the right thing might be to say that 'this is an outstanding performer' and 'let's move that individual on to some other department where we can develop that person' . . . there tends*

*to be a tendency to hold on to those kinds of people in order
to keep your own position firm, to stay in control of your
own position."*

Many resource shortages are illusions. There *are* enough resources to go around. The problem is that too much of the available resource lies dormant or underutilized in some territorial
manager's reserves. The strategy of occupation prevents these
resources from being reallocated. People hoard unconsciously
and automatically. It is a reflex action to grab at what is being
taken away. These players seem to be responding to a vague
"you never know if we might need it" impulse that stimulates
territorial behaviors even when there is no clear source for the
anxiety.

Efficiencies that could be possible through work redesign or
streamlined processes are sabotaged by managers whose fists
are so tightly wrapped around their resources that only plastic
explosives could break their grip. When faced with the inevitably reduced human resource allocations that reengineering
brings to a department manager, the occupation strategy often
surfaces. Managers of reengineered departments often find a
way to hang on to eliminated positions, "occupying" them so
no one else can have them.

*"If a position is eliminated, they like to take that authoriza-
tion and utilize it somewhere else. . . . A couple of positions
were eliminated in the organization because the jobs simply
weren't needed in that particular location anymore. The
manager in this case argues very, very firmly that 'even
though I don't need those authorizations here at this particular location, I want to keep those and use them somewhere
else. I want to create a new job somewhere else and give that
level position to someone else in my organization.' The outcome is that you're in limbo. He wants to hang on . . . it's
still an open issue. It's been going on for over a year now."*

The irrational sabotages the rational. Illusions of reengineered efficiencies vaporize when hoarding prevents the actual
reallocation of those resources. Many organizations have ne-

glected to anticipate the underground territorial strategies that sabotage reengineering efforts.

Occupation as a territorial game circumvents policy, organization charts, and redesigned work flow to draw even more powerful lines of ownership. Seasoned territorial players mock each new organizational design as they use occupation to tighten their hold on valuable resources. Those who play the occupation game as a knee-jerk reaction may seem less possessive than their more thoughtful proactive peers, but the results of the game are the same: mindless grasping.

Gatekeepers

People holding positions of formal authority are not the only players adept at staking out or sandbagging territory. Those who insist on being the only channel for valuable information can bottleneck important processes and prevent progress. The occupation game is most powerful when a player can completely control access. In situations where administrative or technical staff members feel a territorial impulse, the strategy of occupation can wreak havoc on even the best-designed system. In professional firms of lawyers, accountants, or real estate agents, many administrative employees use occupation to accumulate power. Any information of value can be retained and meted out in meager portions along territorial boundaries.

Holding a report, "losing" a telephone message, and playing dumb when asked to source needed information are all examples of how a seemingly "less powerful" member of the team can use occupation strategy to dramatically shift the dynamics of an organization.

It is possible that those occupying the outer levels of an organization are strongly influential in the organization's success or failure through the use of territorial games like the occupation game. In situations where technology has exploded beyond the capacity of any one person, occupation can be particularly powerful at the outer levels. When a technical expert feels threatened, the outcome can be a flustered executive drowning in ignorance while a smug techie looks on in amusement. He has the information and he is going to keep it. It is "his." Denied any other means of enhancing his self-identity, a lesser-paid technical worker will not infrequently turn to occupation to claim a little personal territory all for himself.

Like most territorial games, attempts to enhance personal status in the organization can backfire as others play their games in retaliation. There is no argument that an outer-level employee engaged in this sort of destructive territorial game will eventually "lose." The problem is the loss to the organization in the meantime from a series of tit-for-tat territorial games that take everyone's eyes off the ball.

Gatekeepers occur at all levels of the organization. It is a little more difficult to maneuver complete control of vital information, but not impossible. One software design engineer managed (through energetic hypervigilance) to create a roadblock between his group and the rest of the organization. He was the gatekeeper at the roadblock and he was the only one who knew the password.

> *"He channeled decisions and actions through him(self) so that he could control the time line, so that he could keep the power of the time line as long as possible. He kept people from acting on their own. He controlled the resources and then would decide where the resources went. So if someone went outside what he wanted, they had trouble getting the resources."*

Described as an empire builder, this manager faced the lot of many software design managers. He was constantly pressured to produce code to meet shorter and shorter deadlines. He complained endlessly of a shortage of resources. He was totally unaware that his own occupation game perpetuated the situation. It is reasonable to assume that anxiety or fear drove him to maintain total control of any and all access to his group. Mindlessly occupying the position of gatekeeper, he was locked in a territorial game that defined the rest of the organization as his enemy. As more and more of his time was devoted to protecting his group from these enemies (like MIS, Hardware Design, or the CEO!), less and less of his time was channeled toward designing the product. The game of occupation began to eclipse his focus on doing his job. Eventually he was fired, but the turf battles he created rear their ugly heads to this day.

Preempting Decision Making

Just as with musical chairs, winning the game of occupation can depend on agility and speed. As more decisions are freed from the boundaries of the formal authority of a position, informal access to decision-making authority can leave it open to games-manship. This is not to say that informally made decisions are always influenced by territorial games, but when a game is afoot, watch out. Territorial players vying for the authority to make a decision know that getting there first is the best method.

> *"They preempted a decision and then distributed a memo . . . some people try to assume more responsibility than they actually have. . . . They just bypass the normal channels of authority and take action. If nobody calls them on it, they're successful."*

> *"They basically draw the wagons around and say this is really an internal decision. . . . By drawing the wagons around, they really make the decision themselves . . . so they'll preempt further investigation by making a decision and taking action."*

Evolving from old territorial behaviors designed to protect tangible property or goods, this strategy translates surprisingly well to the intangible. Decision-making responsibility is ex-tremely susceptible to the strategy of occupation. If you have ever missed a meeting at which you were assigned a duty or a task, then you understand occupation. A common strategy is to make a suggestion that X take on a task and then to proceed with that "provisional" assignment throughout the meeting or conversation. Later on, or by the next meeting, X looks very un-cooperative if she doesn't comply. More often than not, the time that this decision "occupied" in people's minds has given it le-gitimacy and X will be expected to provide a damn good reason if she wants to challenge the original decision. Occupation of decision-making authority means sitting in the decision-making chair before anyone else can or does.

In the intangible world, perceptions create reality, so an occupation strategy means creating perceptions of occupation. For decision-making authority, the favorite method these days is to so widely broadcast the decision that rescinding it is close to impossible. Technology comes to the aid of the occupation player with the powerful tool of e-mail. Decisions that are legitimized by memos sent to everyone and anyone that matters are prime examples of occupation. If we go back to the musical chairs metaphor, the wider the distribution list is, the bigger the butt occupying the chair.

Put in a position in which a new structure required new role definitions, one manager of two geographically separated halves of the same department was surprised at the speed at which one department moved to occupy the choicest territory in terms of role responsibility. At this level, the occupation strategy is to begin doing the job, publicize the fact that you are doing it, and soon enough everyone will just assume it was yours in the first place.

> *"They started extending the strategic element into real decisions. They started to crawl into that department's perception of their well-defined role. . . . [One employee] offered to write the first definition of the role on a global basis. I said 'fine.' With that, he wrote it, as you might have expected, much broader. . . . He published it as a document. That gave it legitimacy."*

Monopolizing Your Perceptions

Occupation games occur between individuals, departments, companies, and professions. A doctor described an ongoing turf battle between the fields of podiatry and orthopedics. You may think that you own your body, but take it to a hospital and you will find that it has already been divvied up among all the specialists. In the following situation, the turf under dispute is that area one to four inches above your ankle.

"It is driving the orthopedics nuts. They are saying this is ours. This belongs to us. . . . This manifests itself in journals, publications, . . . the group that publishes the most on a topic begins to create a case for ownership of the subject."

Apparently orthopedics is winning right now. The group has published more and thus occupies the minds of those in the field with the belief that your upper ankle is "theirs." As a matter of fact, your entire body has been claimed by one group or another. Just think about a map of your body with lines of division and flags from each specialty laying claim to your fingers, toes, head, heart, and legs. And you thought they were yours! The "gabby group grabs a piece" simply by virtue of persistence and continued presence. Rational arguments may be part of the never-ending diatribe, but an occupational win is due to the fact that it is never-ending over the appeal of any rational points.

The new flatter organizational structures and the introduction of new group processes carry increased opportunities for political maneuvering. Examples suggest that many task forces, CIT (Continuous Improvement Teams), or other well-intentioned cross-functional teams are operating to create occupancy for an issue, a preferred solution, or even a department's access to resources. The common opinion seems to be that turf mongers can abuse team systems just as easily as they have abused the old hierarchical system. The occupation game works quite well in both systems.

The Occupation Game Self-Test

List the ten top resources that you need in order to do your job. Include the most important relationships that help you achieve your goals. Are you "in" with a particular purchasing agent? Is there an administrative assistant or VP you have spent a lot of time cultivating? Where does your budget come from? What part of it is "yours"? How much can you approve? What valuable information is yours?

Then rate your feelings of territoriality from 1 to 10. Be honest. What resources will you freely share and which are under your complete control?

My Resources	Freely Share	Maintain Complete Control
	2 3 4 5 6 7 8 9	
1. _____	1 —+—+—+—+—+—+—+— 10	
2. _____	1 —+—+—+—+—+—+—+— 10	
3. _____	1 —+—+—+—+—+—+—+— 10	
4. _____	1 —+—+—+—+—+—+—+— 10	
5. _____	1 —+—+—+—+—+—+—+— 10	
6. _____	1 —+—+—+—+—+—+—+— 10	
7. _____	1 —+—+—+—+—+—+—+— 10	
8. _____	1 —+—+—+—+—+—+—+— 10	
9. _____	1 —+—+—+—+—+—+—+— 10	
10. _____	1 —+—+—+—+—+—+—+— 10	

Look at the five resources you want to control the most. Drop the top two. (Some things *need* to be under your complete control.) Now consider the next three. What is the benefit of maintaining complete control for you? for your organization?

_____

_____

_____

How might it negatively affect the organization when you maintain tight control of these resources?

_____

_____

_____

Who might benefit from access to one of these resources? How might the organization benefit if you were to share this resource with that person?

_____

_____

_____

What do you risk by allowing others access to your resource? What advantage do you relinquish? How could you minimize the danger?

_____

_____

_____

_____

5

The Information Manipulation Game

Damned lies and statistics.

We know how powerful information can be. In the seventeenth century Francis Bacon wrote that "knowledge is power." Particularly in our present environment, the responsibility of assembling, interpreting, and formatting information is as powerful as the information itself. More information generates more filters through which the information must pass. Each filter is an opportunity to play the information manipulation game.

Most decisions regarding territory in a corporate environment are based on information of one sort or another. Controlling the information or the interpretation of that information is tantamount to having power over territory. When information itself is the territory, then withholding it would be an occupation game, but in a situation in which the information is used as a tool to protect other territory, the information manipulation game is at play. This means denying a "rival" access to data about resources or information about opportunities. It can mean massaging statistics to send a "tweaked" message favorable to the territorial cause. Manipulating information was the second most frequently cited territorial game described in the research. For those with a territorial urge, "damned lies and statistics" can effectively secure new territory or protect occupied territory—as long as they stay under the surface.

Smiles, Pretending, and Little White Lies

Manipulating or withholding information, while an effective strategy, is not socially desirable. Individuals who overtly withhold information are treated with as much contempt as a kid who hogs all the cookies. So we learned to pretend. Most of us were taught at a very early age to share or at least to look like we were sharing. We learned that if we didn't want to share our cookies we needed to hide some before anyone saw how many we had. You, for instance, may at this very moment have goodies stashed away somewhere so that your spouse or children can't find them. Just a little white lie? Sure. That's what the guy in accounting thinks too as he sits on the trend analysis report that shows his predictions of last year were wrong. The internal justifications for manipulating or withholding information are the key to playing this game successfully. Those most successful at manipulating information have completely convinced themselves that the game is wholly justified.

Withholding information is almost always a covert process with quite elaborate justifications and rationalizations. Since you can rarely be sure when someone is withholding information and since the risk of being branded an accuser can be greater than the damage done through lack of data, most "withholders" succeed in their territorial tactics. But not entirely. They may not get called out on the carpet for their behavior, but people know. They know when others are withholding information about opportunities.

> *"Even though the expertise for a particular project may reside somewhere else in the house, they won't tell them about it. They hide it. Yet, if you ever get into a group meeting and ask somebody if that's going on, the answer will be 'absolutely not.'"*

People manipulate and withhold information every day. In a full-blown territorial dispute, information rarely reaches the other side in its original state. Yet accusations and attacks will only generate denials. In Chapter 16 we discuss how the best counterstrategy is not accusation but a deconstruction of the game player's internal justifications. For now, let's just note that the information manipulation game is always covert and that it is almost always reduced down to "only a little white lie" status in the mind of the game player.

Occupation and Information Manipulation

The occupation game and information manipulation game are often played together. Occupation almost always requires that information be manipulated in order to protect occupied territory. Valuable resources are best protected if they aren't widely perceived as valuable. A diamond is less likely to be stolen if everyone thinks it is just a cubic zircon. Many companies have initiated cross-functional training in an effort to broaden the expertise of their best employees and, funnily enough, to reduce territoriality. But what sounds good in theory does not always transfer to practice. Some managers hide good people so they don't get transferred to another department. Here, one explains how they do it:

> *"The way they hide them is that these are people that work for them so generally they are the ones that are asked about the potential and performance of the individuals. So it's a very easy thing to do—it's not so much what is said but what isn't said about someone. . . . There is still some tendency in some areas to kind of hold on to the best in your organization. They're the ones who support you and make you look good."*

The omission of information seems to be easier to justify internally than out-and-out lying. However, in some cultures providing misleading information is considered to be standard practice. Someone started it, others responded, and eventually the game became a habit of the culture. In an organizational culture where manipulating information is standard practice, the boldness with which one lies is protection enough. In the construction firm described below, good employees are reallocated to fictitious new jobs before anyone else can snap them up.

> *"They will falsify when they are available by absolutely hiding them, by not telling the accurate information. It's a total*

fabrication. They may not have a prayer of getting that job.
They are basically hiding him in the closet, not making him
available."

"Somebody will out and out lie to say this person is not
available or [say] 'I've got to have them.' Everyone in the
meeting knows it's a lie. Absolutely."

Boldness is always a function of a very strong internal justification. You can be sure that the steady-eyed information manipulation player believes she has a right, even an obligation, to
protect something or someone. This is important to remember
when dealing with the information manipulation game. The
game players, in their own mind, are not "really lying." They
are simply doing what they think they have to do in order to
survive. This is how the game, baby step by baby step, gets further and further away from open and honest communication.

Once information manipulation is a corporate-wide game,
the lies get bigger. In one company I worked with, misrepresent-
ing future profits was just another culturally accepted way to
contribute to the Christmas club.

"In order to get a bonus on a job the group will prematurely
estimate the final profit and hide future expenses that will
decrease true profitability. . . . So they paint a rosy picture
and withhold data."

By the time the game reaches this point, an entire corporation can be operating on a 50 percent to 60 percent trust level of
all information circulating within the organization. Imagine the
productivity drain when everyone is convinced that up to half
of the information they receive is pure bull.

Protection From Assistance

The most important information to withhold for any serious territorial player is information that might make the territory look
bad and in need of assistance. To a territorial manager, assistance means invaders. Mindlessly protecting turf from invaders,
a manager in trouble can allow emotion to override rational

thought. Particularly as the situation worsens, distributed information becomes less and less accurate. Panic can escalate information manipulation into a major cover-up. One consulting company engaged to administer an attitude survey found that all of the survey instruments from one particular department were precisely the same.

> *"He had called all his people together and said 'This is how we answer each question.' . . . He saw me [a management consultant] as intruding into his territory and he protected it."*

Even when the group members can figure it out all by themselves, there is a cost. Their creative solution is lost. Other groups facing the same problem must reinvent the wheel. Reading between the lines of the following excerpt, you get the feeling that the individual is speaking not only of others but of his own behavior and his own internal justifications.

> *"Sometimes the problem would go away and you would never know why the problem went away. That was because someone figured out what it was—but they wouldn't tell the rest of us. That's because they didn't want people to know. They would solve their own internal problems without sharing any information. That's because they didn't want blame to be placed. If you're in a blame-placing organization, you may think that you're part of a problem, but you'd never admit that you were part of the problem. You would go and solve the problem, but you would never admit that you solved it."*

This is the territoriality that causes entire divisions to withhold information about mistakes until the whole division is bankrupt rather than risk getting help from outside earlier. Withholding information is usually masked with rationalization and avoidance behaviors or combined with another strategy called confusion or the camouflage game.

In most circumstances, the information is not completely withheld. The cagey information manipulation player offers information with enough spice and finesse that diners hardly notice that it barely resembles its original form.

Brer Rabbit and the Spider

Protecting valued territory is easy with a little information finesse. The laziest territorial players can be the most clever when manipulating information. The Brer Rabbit approach of "please don't throw me in the brier patch" translates into misleadingly negative data about the risks or unattractive aspects of an otherwise attractive bit of turf. A production manager hungering after a new robotics device can complain herself into getting two or three of them. One marketing representative for a telecommunications company told of preparing carefully constructed negative feasibility reports that pointed out all the problems with locating his home office in London. No points for guessing that London is where he wanted to be all along.

The persuasive spider's invitation to the fly is replayed frequently as territorial players spin tales of wealth, glory, and prestige around organizational opportunities that disappear once the contract is signed. The spider version of information manipulation can be played in a variety of situations. An individual on the receiving end of big promises may find himself to be the coveted territory of an ardent game player. Invitations to cooperate in return for promised rewards can ensnare the unwary into an all-out territorial battle that may not be in their or their group's best interests. One brilliant project manager was lured away by a competitor who hoped to cripple the progress of his former employer. None of the big promises materialized. The project manager woke up in a dead-end job, having to start all over again. Older and wiser now, he isn't likely to repeat the same mistake. However, some "flies" never reemerge from the spider's web.

In real life, the manipulation of data is rarely a life-or-death issue. Still, decisions are corrupted by varying degrees of inappropriateness and inaccuracy through manipulated data. How many products do we use that have features that were some product manager's pet idea?

Imagine the design meeting described below. You get the impression that these people need to revisit the fundamental purpose of consumer research. Consumer statistics had clearly indicated that a particular feature was not very important. However, presented along with much less desirable features, the feature was made to appear to be desirable so that it would be retained in the design. There are many stories just like this. It happens everywhere, but no one wants to call it for what it is. Notice that the speaker is squeamish about even using the word *manipulated.*

> *"Another example is where data can be selectively manipulated. That's a strong word for what I'm describing, but I've seen instances where selective use of data can basically get you to a different conclusion. They are protecting their own territory. The conclusion they're going for—let's assume we're looking at a particular feature on a product. It's a strong desire from one group in the company to have this feature. Another group . . . may not feel it's that important. . . . It becomes a judgment call. You are adding cost, adding weight. The one that wants the feature will tend to collect data and present data that would enhance the attractiveness of that feature. On the other hand, other people will be tweaking the numbers the other way."*

Here, the territorial battle has escalated beyond rational evaluation. A feature has now become intertwined with each group's perception of its "authority" territory. Personal feelings get involved and no one seems overly concerned with the consumer's needs. Winning the point overshadows the original objective.

> *"The response when tweaking numbers is that they're doing what the system allows them to do. They feel, 'I'm within the rules. I'm applying the rules to my benefit, but I'm still playing within the rules.' "*

The game continues because people can claim that they are playing "within the rules." It is justifiable because everyone does it. It is justifiable because it is labeled "tweaking" rather than "manipulating." Notice that *tweaking* is a much more popular term than *manipulation.* Listening to the justifications is just as informative as recognizing the games. The justification is the most important part of the game to understand. It will be the target of your efforts when you set out to reduce some of these games.

Baffling the Opposition

Manipulating information is easier when the situation is complex. Today, many decisions founder in the seas of seemingly relevant information. The territorial player who wants to manipulate information is at a significant advantage in this environment. Smart players know that too much information is a brilliant way of hiding information damaging to the territorial cause. This tactic plays to the vanity of others. Few people are going to admit that they don't understand the data. Their reluctance to ask questions paves the way for the game.

> *"When you design a car, there are 25,000 parts in a car. The way those parts go together changes. Let's say, hypothetically, half of them are changed so that it's easier to put them together and 40 percent stay the same and 10 percent are harder to put together, [they] take more time. They can go through that 10 percent and create data which say that [that] 10 percent cause the car to take another hour and a half to put together. They create data, then they'll go through and say, 'Well, we took these other actions that reduce the cost of putting it together and we'll give them a big list of that.' Then they'll say, 'Well, we've looked at it, and it takes an hour longer to put it together.' They create and control the data. When they control the data, you can never end up in the final analysis winning an argument. So then their estimate goes on the books."*

"Their" win is simply a matter of presenting too much information arranged in a way that discourages analysis. It gets filed in the "too hard" basket. Just like the employees in Chapter 2 who pictured their organization in an ocean of information, many territorial games thrive on the current proliferation of information. The needle in the haystack remains successfully hidden by an astute information manipulation game player.

What Elephant?

A twist on hiding information is the tactic of hiding *from* information. Less often, but just as destructively, territorial players will seek to exclude information from outside sources. Suppressing information can take many forms. Other territorial games like the intimidation game (Chapter 6) or the discredit game (Chapter 10) can be very effective in preventing others from bringing in new information. And yet the simplest form of manipulating information that is trying to find its way "in" is to refuse to listen. In a meeting, for instance,

> *"you can tell—what you see are facial expressions, folded arms. They close themselves off. You conclude that they disagree with something or they don't want to hear something. They nonverbally close off the input."*

Recently it has been popular to say that all humans automatically resist change. In the paradigm of territoriality, humans don't resist *all* change. They resist changes that might threaten their territory. Any reduction in jurisdiction, freedom, or control is likely to instigate the "shut down" form of the information manipulation game.

> *"So you have a team meeting and you're saying, 'Look, guys, can't we reduce the number of prototypes?' The answer is never, 'OK, let's look at that' or 'Let's look at the possibilities.' It's always, 'No, you can't do that; it's not the way it's been done, it's not the way we're going to do it.' All conversation stops at that point. We used to call these chimneys. . . . Nowadays we are trying not to develop chimneys, but we still have our old behavior."*

The jargon that has developed to describe this behavior always recalls narrow exclusive structures. We call them chimneys or silos because trying to get information *in* to the department that has built a wall around itself is like trying to throw a sack of grain into a silo fifty feet high with a diameter of only ten feet. What's the use of trying? So everyone ends up with a distorted, incomplete picture of reality.

Even when new organizational structures discourage internal boundaries, the "old behaviors" continue. This is because the behavior is more a function of an internal territorial urge than of any imposed divisions. Remove the divisions and people just build new ones. People always reduce their world down to their definition of relevant and irrelevant. The boundaries of what is relevant define their territory and fuel their games.

Understanding the territory that lies outside the boundaries is as important as knowing what lies within the boundaries. Problems in organizations arise just as often when individuals *don't* take ownership as when they do. Saying "That's not my problem" is just another way of playing the information manipulation game.

> *"So you've got a subculture that is trying to go for their optimum, which is counter to the big-picture good. . . . What actually happens in the interchange from human to human is that they refuse to look at the big picture. They tell you flat out in a meeting. I've made the request that we look at the big picture and their response back is that they don't get measured to do that, not paid to do that. I'm measured on meeting this objective and that's what I'm talking to you about."*

For individuals concerned about protecting their territory, certain information can be scary. Playing the information manipulation game protects a territorial player from hearing or revealing scary information. Unfortunately, this game "protects" everyone else from what might be vital information necessary to the organization's success.

Talking about this game is made more difficult because the manipulation of information can grease the wheels of an organization as well as jam them. Little white lies are necessary to all aspects of our social interactions. Anyone who has ever been asked, "Does this dress make me look fat?" knows that. Assuring peers that the boss loved the presentation, sitting on a customer complaint that might be blown out of proportion—these things are necessary. The truly honest don't survive in organizations. However, the truly paranoid or overly acquisitive territorial players take little white lies to a game level that can threaten the organization's survival.

THE INFORMATION MANIPULATION GAME SELF-TEST

Rate the confidence level for information, in general, across your organization. How much of the information is trusted as accurate, open, and honest?   90 percent __   70 percent __   50 percent __   less __

If you feel that less than 80 percent of the information is trusted, what is the cost to your organization?

_____

_____

_____

Think about the big decisions that get made in your organization—e.g., decisions on capital budgeting, computer system changes, product development, or research and development investments. List below the information that is most important to these decisions. List the information that wields power. Get specific. Don't just list "accounting information." Describe it. Is it the quarterly sales figures segmented by region? The net profit ratios? Or is it the scrap or overflow inventory calculations?

After you have listed them, write the name of the person or department responsible for the preparation and dissemination of that information.

Powerful Information	Information Delivery/Preparation Points
1. _____	1. _____
2. _____	2. _____
3. _____	3. _____
4. _____	4. _____
5. _____	5. _____
6. _____	6. _____
7. _____	7. _____

If your name came up, have you *ever* put a spin on information? Did you *ever* orchestrate the timing of the delivery of data to achieve some purpose?

_____

_____

_____

If so, what was the positive outcome of that situation?

_____

_____

_____

How might this have had a negative impact on another part of the organization?

_____

_____

_____

Are there other instances where you think information is being manipulated? If so, what territory is the manipulator trying to protect with this game?

_____

_____

How do you think that person would answer the previous questions?

_____

_____

_____

_____

_____

6

The Intimidation Game

"Make my day."

The territorial game most firmly grounded in our animal instincts is the intimidation game. Think back to the time when cavemen and women had just figured out that if they could keep a particularly rich hunting ground for themselves, life would be easier. Keeping it for themselves meant keeping others out. Lacking handy NO TRESPASSING signs, they developed behaviors that were designed to let outsiders know they weren't welcome. Growling worked pretty well. So did posting the disembodied skulls of those unfortunates who had committed the ultimate faux pas of overstepping their boundaries. Originally, the focus was on scaring the bejesus out of anyone even considering a trespass into their territory. As time went on, the marking of boundaries turned into the psychological game of intimidation.

Even in the animal kingdom, territorial animals that fight over territory rarely fight to the death. Instead they fight mock battles designed to intimidate would-be invaders from trying again. The success of the mockingbird in protecting territory illustrates that battles need not be fatal. Birds can play the intimidation game with animals of much greater strength and size. Cats and people (myself included) will respect a vigilant mockingbird intent on playing the intimidation game through mock battles.

Our corporate culture is full of these mock battles. Corporate jargon has evolved the richly descriptive phrase of a "pissing contest" to describe the status-defining mock battles that mark and defend psychological territory. Many of the mock battles in corporate land are not so different from those battles we see on a *National Geographic* special between moose, antelope, or lions. While you might not see antlers locked in a head-butting contest at a meeting of a newly formed task team, there are other behaviors that serve the same purpose.

Snarling and Growling

Imagine walking up to a really mean dog (a really *big* mean dog) while he is eating and listening as you get nearer and nearer to his bowl. You would probably hear a noise designed by nature to discourage further progress. If this were real life, you might even notice a physiological response in your own body—perhaps a quickening of the heart rate or a little shot of fear up the spine. This growl can have the same physiological effect on you as a real attack.

However, growling is not an attack. It requires no more movement than vibrating vocal chords and a curled lip. It is simply a warning system. But because it warns of an attack, the corresponding emotional reaction can sometimes be the same as if an attack were actually in progress. Reaction to a growl does not require a conscious thought. It is automatic. It is a limbic system reaction. Literally before you know it, you've got a tight gut sensation. In fact, it takes conscious thought to override the automatic reaction to a serious growl.

The intimidation game can work just like this. Of course, most people don't actually growl. But people have their own warning systems. Raised voices, lowered voices, raised eyebrows, lowered eyebrows, tapping fingers impatiently—it's different for everyone. People just use whatever worked before. The common element is the escalation of some behavior as a warning.

Anger or frustration, annoyance, whatever you want to call it is the source emotion for intimidation. This emotion can infuse any behavior with an intimidation message. A waiter serving a cup of tea with the right amount of force and a good dose of attitude qualifies. It is not what is said or what is done, but *how* it is said or done.

In the corporate game a smart player will be very subtle. The art of intimidation in the corporate world requires that intimidation adequately fit, if only barely, within the limits of civilized social intercourse. It is easy to imagine the following "professional conversation," with each speaker carefully staying well within the bounds of polite discourse as they played the intimidation game:

> *"Voices were raised. I was angry, but it was a 'professional' conversation. The message I was sending him is that 'you don't know what you're talking about and that's not your decision to make.' It got tabled, then assigned to someone else, and a verbal warning was delivered about not doing it again. My territory was being approached and I responded with a strong, verbal 'back-off' message."*

Intimidation between peer levels usually generates a stronger signal. Superior-to-subordinate communications can use much more subtle levels of the intimidation game. A strongly territorial manager can train his subordinates, as in the following example, to "shut down" with only the slightest intimidation warning.

> *"I've observed in meetings that key managers or top managers in an organization—particularly when they've got subordinates in the room—can be very intimidating. If they don't like what they are hearing, they will give either verbal or body language to their people. Rather than pursue a particular point, the subordinate will shut down. Some signals are furrowed brows, narrowed eyes, shaking the head back and forth, or even saying, 'What in the hell are you talking about?' So they effectively shut down somebody . . . they feel threatened as a result of what they say."*

Ideas are lost, alternatives left unexplored, and cautions unheard because of an intimidation game that better reflects the psychological needs of the manager than the current needs of the organization. Many powerful people in organizations justify their intimidation games through some outdated theory that it "keeps people on their toes." On the contrary, people are probably more productive when they have both feet firmly on the ground. Playing the intimidation game only makes people jumpy and allows the game player a perverse pleasure in protecting his turf by keeping others off balance.

An Offer They Can't Refuse

The intimidation game sometimes looks like an intricate dance. In the movie *The Godfather*, the character Don Corleone mixes a strange combination of seductiveness and threat to create a profoundly intimidating effect. Veiled threats work quite well in intimidating others away from valued territory. On the surface, everything looks normal, but the target of the intimidation game is receiving the message loud and clear. The following example demonstrates a situation where the surface interaction is in direct contradiction to the private message being sent.

These two department heads have made a public agreement to share limited resources, but one of them has no intention of following through on the deal. Agreement is friendly and generous until the two approach the practical aspects of sharing the services of a group of administrative staff.

> *"I say, 'OK, I'll use Jeff and Bob for this project,' but that encroaches on his territory. His reaction is to escalate with a threat that, 'If you do that, I'll have to take Sue back for my project.' Therefore, there is no actual agreement in practice. It's a tit-for-tat battle over limited resources."*

This was a private conversation. This level of the intimidation game usually requires privacy. Threats of extreme inconvenience, like invoking an agonizingly detailed policy that is ignored by the rest of the company, can be as effective in a corporate turf battle as placing a bloody horse head in someone's bed. Even more subtle than veiled threats is the intimidation game variation called sarcasm.

Sarcasm: Anger in a Clown Suit

One of the most powerful forms of intimidation is public humiliation. It is also one of the easiest to get away with. A casually surprised, "Wassa matter, can't take a joke?" can brand the target as "oversensitive" or worse, one who "takes everything personally."

Territorial players can scare others off by making them look stupid in front of their peers, superiors, or subordinates. Even a well-placed jab in front of strangers is enough to make some people back down. This strategy is very close to the discredit strategy (Chapter 10), but sarcasm is more of a personal attack than an attempt to discredit the validity of another's input. To the target it feels like an act of aggression, not humor. Like the other territorial strategies, sarcasm thrives beneath a cloak of rationalization. Take, for instance, the story passed down about this manager, who probably perceived himself as merely introducing new policies. Yet if he had been solely concerned with the new policies, he would have omitted the floor show.

> *"So at a staff meeting, with a number of other managers, Joe, the new manager, says to Mick that he noticed there was a request here to put a new roof on such and such property in X town. He says, 'Tell me how you would go about doing that.' Mick goes through how he would do it. And Joe says, 'That's how you used to do it when you ran the show, but that's not how we do it anymore. Get out your notebook and take close notes. I'm about to tell you how we are going to do things going forward.' The story goes that one of the other managers had to literally hold Mick down in his seat."*

Giggles from his compatriots escalated the exaggerated performance of this territorial manager. The humiliation experienced was enough to make Mick resign. This turned out to be a very successful territorial game for Joe. Mick was excluded not only from the territory but from the entire company. Milder versions of sarcasm can have milder effects, but sarcasm rarely promotes cooperation. Hiding under the auspices of humor, sarcasm is merely anger in a clown suit employed to deliver a message of superior power to anyone who would challenge it.

The message is, effectively: Mess with my territory and risk being made a fool of. That's pretty intimidating, particularly to an otherwise competent manager who is not so good at verbal volleys.

Letting Her Rip

Sometimes the emotions kick in with such force that a territorial player momentarily forgets the societal injunctions against verbal onslaughts. We usually call this "losing it." A person need only "lose it" once to effectively prevent any further intrusions into his or her territory. The following description is a good example of an emotional hijacking of the rational brain. This normally mild-mannered guy has just been confronted with a decision, made by him, that had been very bad for the organization. His territory was in big danger, and the emotion flooding his words reflects his limbic system's reaction to this danger.

> *"All of a sudden he flared into a defensive kind of maneuver. He lapsed into another language. It was uncharacteristic of the guy. He turned crimson. He was saying, 'I made the decision. It was my judgment to make.' Underneath all that, I was hearing, 'Look, back off. Stay out of my turf, regardless of the data.'"*

Anger not only floods the threatened individual's body with adrenaline; a strong display will activate everyone else too. Recently, I was asked to intervene with a computer design team whose head hardware and software engineers frequently employed extreme expressions of anger in a back-and-forth intimidation game that, for them, had lasted for years. Tempers would flare, four-letter words would fly, and the two would engage in a screaming match that could be heard for miles. Both engineers were totally unaware that each outburst stopped work for up to half an hour. After the screaming stopped, the rest of the team nervously giggled or discussed the display until their own heart rates calmed down and they could return their attention to the work at hand. The expression of strong emotion travels through a group and stirs up reactive emotions in everyone. Think about how much productive time was lost every time these guys threw one of their hissy-fits.

At its most extreme level, the intimidation game arises when the territorial situation is at its least rational point. Faced with invading consultants who were suggesting a "better way," this old-school manager became flooded with enough emotion to cut off his rational processes:

> *"That's when the nerve was hit. He was angry. His face got red. Then he became accusatory, belligerent. He said he thought that the people who had done the study didn't know what they were doing. He sat in judgment. They finished their presentation and left the room and that was the end of it, period. It was never to be discussed again. . . . The outcome, in my opinion, was that the subordinates of the manager involved said, 'Well, it looks like we don't go out and ask anybody questions like that anymore.' . . . What a lot of money ended up in the wastebasket. It diminished the future flow of information. It negated some really useful information. There were areas that may have been closed off altogether. Because they saw this reaction, they knew that there were some areas they would not get into with him."*

The worst part of the intimidation game is that the reaction of others witnessing it is rarely rational either. People can be permanently backed down by means of a powerful outburst. Not because of a rational evaluation but because powerful emotion has been so strongly encoded in their memory that the very thought of going "there" again arouses negative feelings that skew rational thinking processes. They probably don't feel fear, exactly. It is more of a feeling that it is just not worth the trouble.

Ensuring That "It's Just Not Worth It"

The net effect of intimidation is that the perceived territorial "invader" is scared off, not only at the time of the exchange but, ideally, for good. This is not to say that the intimidation game always uses fear to repel invaders. Sure, some methods of intimidation evoke a version of fear. Others need only be annoying.

Intimidation does not require the intimidator to hold a position of power.

On the contrary, I've seen a two-man maintenance staff protect territory from employees who were supposed to command twice the organizational power. Perhaps the tattoos and the Harleys in the parking lot helped, but these men had the rest of the staff trained. They required common rooms to be locked at all times. Use of the room was officially free to everyone. All an employee needed to do was ask for a key. But finding someone to ask for a key, explaining the need for the room, and following him to the room once access was granted built up an intimidation effect that probably cut use of the rooms in half. These rooms were the maintenance men's turf, and it's easier to clean an unused room. No question that the system was fair and reasonable on the surface. In this case, the intimidation operated below the surface. The intimidation game is a function of tone and manner more than content.

Therefore, intimidation need only generate a response that is some version of "it's just not worth the trouble." Accounting departments can use the intimidation game to control expense decisions by intimidating other employees when they hand in their expense reports. One popular *Dilbert* cartoon characterizes this situation when the expense account filer must endure fire, brimstone, and the challenge of presenting the head of a coworker on a platter before the expense report is approved. All the intimidator need do is escalate to the point where "it's just not worth it" for the other person.

Subtle cues communicate these warnings. The following excerpt is a remarkably detailed observation that describes behaviors we usually read and respond to unconsciously. Notice how the intimidation rises and falls as the speaker approaches and retracts from the territorial subject. This is the same methodology used in behaviorism. It may be a primitive method, but most of the time it works very, very well.

> *"What I observed was a rising annoyance and a change in eye contact . . . not shifty-eyed (he's not like that)—he avoided eye contact. His voice changed. It got slightly more shrill for lack of a better word. It got a little higher in the sinus cavity . . . he was a little more flushed—[it was] a little*

> *more clinched kind of communication style. . . . Then I*
> *backed down, he subsided, and we parted. I decided that this*
> *is not a hill I'm going to die on. It's a nice opportunity,*
> *but . . ."*

In organizations, the intimidation game works well because there are plenty of hills not worth dying for. Particularly when an organization has a bad case of apathy, the intimidation game can kill any glimmer of initiative. Territory can be protected by as little effort as a wide-eyed "What did you say?!"

Crossing the Styx

The intimidation game can draw territorial boundaries that last for decades. Corporate culture is full of stories and company myths that are designed to let newcomers know which groups "own" which territory. As with the myth of Charon ferrying dead souls over the River Styx, crossing over certain boundaries might mean that you are never seen or heard from again. These stories can be repeated with an echo of the original intimidation that warns newcomers to "keep off." Raised eyebrows and warnings of "you don't want to do that" delivered in a tone usually reserved for warnings about haunted houses effectively protect territory. Territory can be protected long after the original territorial player has gone.

In a factory, stories are passed down in a modern-day version of the oral history. Some stories are repeated to new workers in the natural process of showing them the ropes. Outbursts make good stories. One outburst can live for decades. It can even grow with time. Entire divisions become effectively cordoned off as restricted territory.

One example of an old territorial boundary placed years ago through a single intimidation game involves a worker whose production line could have been twice as productive. A passing consultant noticed an obvious fault and asked why he had not reported it. The worker responded that he *had* reported the fault a couple of years ago and the manager had shut him down sufficiently to keep him quiet for two years:

"He said when he wanted something from me, he would ask me. I decided to mind my own business."

Territorial boundaries, once defined, can be respected indefinitely. Once one person runs into them and gets a bloody nose, word spreads. Word of danger seems to travel wider and faster than other news. Old battles are remembered for a long, long time.

Depending on the culture of the organization, intimidation can take many forms: veiled threats, public humiliation, verbal violence, or some other form of scare tactic. The net effect is to cordon off an area of information, relationships, or decision-making authority on the basis of Darwin's rules rather than any rational evaluation of how best to serve the organization's purpose. Old boundaries can last for years, sabotaging opportunities for cooperation.

THE INTIMIDATION GAME SELF-TEST

Following are ten intimidation tactics. Circle the three you use most frequently.

1. Talking louder
2. Slamming things around
3. Holding a sustained stare
4. Verbal warnings or clear counterattacks
5. Interrogating questions
6. Talking softer, more deliberately
7. Head shaking, huffs, eye rolling
8. Sarcasm
9. Flashes of anger
10. Meaningful silences

Describe the last time you used one of these behaviors to make a point. What were you protecting? From whom? Did it work?

_____

_____

What unintended effect might still operate as a result of this behavior?

_____

_____

Now consider what might have happened if you had not used this behavior. What might have been a positive outcome for the organization as a whole?

_____

_____

What would have been the negative outcome? Was there another way to avoid this negative outcome?

_____

_____

7

The Powerful Alliances Game

Friends in high places.

The old adage "It's not what you know, but who you know" is a core truth in territorial warfare. Savvy executives build allies and/or plant spies in critical places in the organization and in the industry. If that sounds distastefully manipulative, consider your own efforts to make friends with your boss's secretary, do a favor for a peer, or make offerings of donuts or cookies to the administrative staff or the accounting department. Sure, it's "just good business," relationship building, and in normal circumstances these relationships contribute to the success of the organization. In fact, powerful alliances are absolutely necessary in today's business environment. Those people who can pick up the phone and ask a favor of just about anyone are the movers and shakers who build successful organizations. They can also bring them down.

Any alliance that can be placed in the category of "good" territoriality can just as well be used in a territorial game. An overactive territorial impulse can transform a network of peers into one long boa constrictor squeezing the life out of a perceived invader.

When a turf war erupts, people choose sides. Whether they are aware of it or not, relationship building comes into play. Rationally, they may deny that an individual's interest in his kids or the free tickets to a ball game have anything to do with choosing a side, but these things have everything to do with it. This isn't lost on those prone to playing territorial games. The powerful alliances game drives a territorial player to build alliances. Players may or may not be conscious that the originating impulse comes from the territorial drive. Like all the other games, the powerful alliances game is easy to justify after the fact.

Much like the U.S. Defense Department's bases located on foreign soil, "ally agreements," or a cooperative alliance between unions, powerful alliances give those engaged in them extra clout and maneuverability to protect their territory. Having powerful alliances in the corporate arena protects intangible territory. There are many good examples of powerful alliances having served the organization's purpose, but there are just as many bad examples in which internal turf wars over subterritories were won by means of powerful alliances at great expense to the organization. Company policies that limit nepotism are in direct response to some of the powerful alliances that can allow territorial goals to eclipse organizational goals.

Visualize an organization chart for your organization, one that might be published in a company document. Now, in your mind's eye, take some colored pencils: blue for strong alliances, green for moderate alliances, and red for antagonistic relationships. Try to draw the "real" power structure of your organization. Since information is power, consider the practical lines of information flow. Information rarely flows in a way that reflects the organization chart. What lines would you draw to indicate the more realistic information flow channels of country clubs, golf games, or sailing buddies? Is anyone related? Who took a fall for someone else lately? Who knows all the dirt? Who is sleeping with whom? Who *used* to be sleeping with whom?

A recent TV sitcom devoted an entire episode to a hapless manager who inadvertently fired the boss's mistress. Anticipating his own impending unemployment, he railed, "These people ought to wear signs on their foreheads!" Powerful alliances operate to create channels of information, to affect decision making, and to create other relationships very useful in protecting territory. Ignore them at your peril.

As with the information manipulation game, if the relationship constitutes the "turf," then protecting that relationship is the occupation game. For instance, if being buddies with the CEO is valued simply by virtue of the prestige it offers, then the relationship itself is protected as an intangible territory. However, when the protected turf is something like a project, access to resources, or an ego attachment to a particular marketing strategy, then establishing or tapping into relationships for the purpose of protecting that turf is playing the powerful alliances game. When blended into perfectly acceptable friendship behavior, this game can be very subtle. Yet observers are very aware when it is in play.

Brownnosers

Most of the individuals interviewed displayed a general disdain for the brownnoser. The stories told to describe this practice did not really identify any behaviors that were offensive per se. In fact, brownnose behaviors could objectively be categorized as courteous, polite, diplomatic, and even respectful. The descriptions centered more on *how* these behaviors were used. No self-respecting brownnoser is going to be obvious! The brownnoser uses only socially acceptable behaviors. However, unlike a polite or particularly diplomatic employee, the brownnoser is jockeying for position (territory) in a way that pushes others out or down. The brownnoser turns relationship building into a territorial game when she perceives another's gain as her loss. One trait of a brownnoser is a telltale grin when a peer loses his thought or makes a mistake. For her, it is a win/lose game over finite territory.

Coming from a territorial perspective, building alliances is a game to be won or lost using strategy and conscious effort. The research produced stories of brownnosers that centered around the calculated use of relationship-building techniques. The most offensive aspect seemed to be the lack of genuine affection involved. They were considered to be fakers.

> *"He would meet with the boss when no one else was around. He would speak one-on-one. He would kind of try to position himself as being the* most *successful of all the direct reports. He was making and building alliances. He would even get to*

*the point of going beyond his boss to the VP. There he could
build relationships with them."*

One observer interviewed described an eloquent speaker
who was presenting only "half the story" and charming people
(owners of turf that he wanted) with the charisma of his delivery. While charisma is a highly desirable trait, in a territorial
game it can overpower other, less charismatic employees who
may have a better handle on the organization's needs and goals.
The brownnoser in this case

*"had been doing behind-the-scenes negotiating and lining up
of strategies with all his colleagues back at his home base."*

Lost in the game, this territorial player effectively blocked
an initiative that might have saved the company a lot of money.
Unfortunately for the company, he perceived that it would cost
him valuable territory. So he played the powerful alliances game
and kept that territory for himself.

Sleepers

The development of powerful alliances depends on the influence
the alliance is willing or able to wield. Territorial players usually
pick their battles. Because most employees of an organization
have a conscious desire to help the organization succeed, territorial games are usually fought in small skirmishes, like guerrilla
warfare. This makes it easier for everyone to pretend they aren't
playing games. It also means that those recruited through powerful alliances can have absolutely no idea that they are collud-
ing in a territorial game. Upon reflection, they might not have
chosen to play, but there is usually not a lot of reflection going
on. Organizational games can escalate with the same speed as a
food fight in a high school cafeteria.

Once in the skirmish, people's emotions are stirred and they
get caught up in the rationalizations for the game. Soon they are
playing with the same intensity as the originator. These people
who originally had no vested interest in the territory are like
sleepers. The sleeper is jolted into mindless action by a game

player who, at some point, forged an alliance and created enough of a sense of obligation to fuel a response. The nicest technical support person you could ever hope to meet, after a phone call from his buddy on the company basketball team, can slide a purchase request to the bottom of the pile and never really know why he did it.

In a recent merger, territorial feelings were running high. A new manager from the other company was asked to take over a department. One of the previously powerful veteran employees had activated every sleeper from her old department to "freeze out" the new manager. The veteran's allies began to actively engage in their own territorial strategies, such as strategic noncompliance (Chapter 9) and shunning (Chapter 11), as a result of the alliance.

> *"The veteran had a lot of people on her side. . . . The veteran's cohorts were sending the message that even though their boss was saying do this and do that, they wouldn't do it."*

If we questioned each of these people who were acting on the "side" of the veteran, they would all have a reasonable justification for rebelling against the new manager. Very few of them would be aware that they might actually be responding to a mindless sense of obligation or to some primitive urge to protect a fellow "insider." Once the battle is in full swing, people rarely take time to reflect on how they were recruited.

Strange Bedfellows

Territorial games can be fought and won exclusively through office politics. In fact, each game could just as well be labeled a political strategy. My choice to observe these behaviors through the lens of the territorial drive changes the view a bit, but the subject is the same. When people are engaged in office politics, they are incorporating the game of powerful alliances. And that means forming relationships based not on friendship, shared ideology, or affection but purely on a need to protect desired territory. Strange bedfellows indeed.

Powerful alliances mean access to borrowed power. Coalitions between two groups or two individuals can wield more power than either one can alone. Each cuts a deal that protects its territory or pushes its agenda, and attention to the original goal slips away.

Apparently the fields of psychiatry and psychology have been fighting over psychiatry's exclusive privilege of prescribing medicine. With new, safe drugs becoming more important in psychological treatment, the psychologists think they should share the privilege of prescribing certain drugs. After using the occupation game of publishing and widely distributing information, both decided to enhance their position through the strategy of forging powerful alliances. Psychiatry courted the neurosurgeons while psychology went after other professions likely to be sympathetic.

> *"They would do things that made them more embedded with their brethren in neurosurgery and what have you. . . . They wanted to build major alliances. As a matter of fact, what psychology would do is align itself with optometry, nursing, pharmacy. . . . Nursing was incredibly powerful. They [nurses] already had statutes to prescribe in a lot of states."*

No doubt some of this conflict took the high road and was always focused on the needs of patients. However, it is a safe bet that deals were struck, promises made, and personal agendas pursued. For some of those involved, the issue of prescribing medicine was just as much a clash of egos (psychological territory) as a concern for patient health. Each side would vehemently argue that its efforts were driven by a concern for patients' welfare. No one can argue with that. But no one really believes it either. Whatever the reason, each field sought to protect (or invade) the "right to prescribe" turf, and they both used the powerful alliances game as a primary strategy.

Shoulder Rubbing

Understanding the powerful alliances game means understanding the role of face-to-face contacts. Frequent interactions can create powerful connections between people even when there is no intention of building an alliance. As mentioned in discussing the occupation game, executives usually underestimate the power of frequent face-to-face interactions. That oversight can have territorial consequences.

The following example describes a territorial battle initiated by a woman, Claire, who was after her manager's job. She was very clear about that. She was more or less honest in the way she set about winning the coveted title. First, she increased her interactions with everyone else in the department. Through sheer persistence, she began building alliances. Her manager, Vicky, watched it happening:

> *"The way the office is set up—I can't see my department from where I sit so Claire had a workstation a couple of aisles down and what she did, in essence, she became very close to one of the individuals, who then acted like whatever I said had absolutely no merit. He began to only listen to what Claire said. Claire also began isolating the other individuals who were in that area. She could have a lot of face-to-face contact that I couldn't match."*

Vicky was fast losing ground because the game being played by her unhappy subordinate began to erode her own relationships. This territorial rival was after Vicky's job, and she used the powerful alliances game not only with her peers but with Vicky's boss.

> *"My boss had an open door policy, and Claire would walk in there and would attack me—not a conversation, an attack. After a while I think he started to believe it."*

This stopped being an effective tool with the arrival of a new boss who encouraged people to use the established lines of communication. Claire, no longer able to use the powerful alliances game to invade authority turf lines, soon resigned. However, the game might have worked. In a complex world, a boss must struggle to distinguish between important data from a conscientious employee and deliberate misinformation from a jealous/slighted/paranoid employee—particularly when that employee seems to be a willing and able ally.

Almost everyone who hears this story assumes that they wouldn't be "taken in" by this sort of game. They underestimate the power of frequent interactions. Perhaps there is a physiological basis for the phenomenon, but it seems that constant contact with another human being can forge a sense of kinship that will override organizational charts. If you haven't talked to your network of alliances lately, someone else probably has.

Monopolizing "Face Time"

Sometimes establishing a powerful alliance can be a function of deemphasizing the importance, value, or contributions of others. In one situation, Laura, an account manager at an accounting firm, had a young performer, Tony, on whom the client relied more and more for strategic advice. As Laura felt her powerful alliances with key decision makers diminishing, she began to show up unannounced at more meetings. She would call the client for meetings, exclude Tony, and insist that all correspondence be filtered through her—with her signature. Good news was delayed until she could deliver it personally. She grabbed every opportunity, and even created more, to build a powerful alliance with the client's representative. The problem was that she was grabbing a good relationship from her own employee.

Laura made no effort to increase the value provided the client, only to increase the frequency of contact. This was a purely territorial game. The result was a demoralized, increasingly apathetic employee. More and more of Laura's productive time was wasted hovering over the client. And the client found it hard not to notice her insecurities.

Laura probably believed she was doing her job instead of mindlessly responding to internal fear messages. Because powerful alliances can be such an important element in doing a good job, the game is easily justified. Despite the rationalizations that often accompany it, most astute corporate observers are very aware when this game is in play. In some cases, the people excluded are more important than those included.

> *"A specific example would be in meetings where a lot of time is spent on who attends the meeting. It isn't always territo-*

rial in the sense of we're sales and marketing and we don't
want someone from, let's say, purchasing to be in this meet-
ing. It's territorial in a multifaceted way. It could be territo-
rial like we, the chief engineers, . . . don't want anyone below
us. . . . People are excluded to protect territory."

What is going on here? The chief engineers have excluded
anyone subordinate to their position from a meeting. Why?
There could be a very good reason, but the person interviewed
described it as a "territorial reason." Perhaps powerful alliances
are eroded by the "less important." Maybe there is less competition without the subordinates in the room. It doesn't matter.
None of those reasons has anything to do with designing a better product. The game grabbed attention away from the goal.

That is the danger in all these games, particularly the powerful alliances game. It is so difficult to determine when the behavior has shifted into a game. The powerful alliances game was
one of the few games that interviewees frequently mentioned as
a strategy they used themselves. It seems to have fewer negative
connotations than the rest of the games. Because it is so often
used in the development of "good" territoriality, more people
are willing to report it. One executive began describing his tried-
and-true formula for getting things done:

"The next thing I do is find out if there are allies out there
that really support my view."

Indeed the establishment of powerful alliances is not always
a game. Yet there are always clues. A game is best identified
by the results. At the game level, the powerful alliances game
interrupts or even blocks the flow of information. Team effectiveness is damaged by resentment and blame behavior. Whenever
building an alliance becomes a competitive endeavor, you can
be sure you are playing a game. The challenge is to determine
when you have stopped using your network of contacts for the
organization's good and instead started using your powerful alliances to protect psychological turf of your own.

THE POWERFUL ALLIANCES GAME SELF-TEST

Let's do more than visualize the exercise. Get an "official" organization chart for your group or draw your own here. Make it broad enough to encompass all the important relationships, up, down, and sideways. Find some colored pens and diagram the relationships as best you can, using blue for strong relationships, green for moderate relationships, and red for those that are antagonistic.

Who is tied to you by a red line?

_____

_____

_____

Who is strongly associated with the ones with whom you have a red-line relationship?

_____

_____

_____

How does this affect your relationship with those people?

_____

_____

_____

Of your strong (blue) relationships, look at the people with whom they have antagonistic (red) relationships. How does this affect your relationships with these people?

_____

_____

_____

If you find that you and the rest of your blue-line buddies share the same red lines, describe the lines of division in terms of turf. What area, turf, or position do they represent and what side do you represent?

What would be the effect if you could merge each "side" into one team? (Don't worry about it being "impossible." Just describe the impact.)

8

The Invisible Wall Game

It must be the gremlins.

Imagine the following scenario. You are in charge of a critical project. You have identified the critical path for implementation. The action plan is under way, but for some reason nothing is going as planned. You "just can't win for losing." Everything that has gone wrong has a perfectly logical reason, and yet . . . something just doesn't feel right. You can't quite put your finger on it, but you have a distinct feeling that the problems are due to more than just coincidence. If this has ever happened to you, chances are that the crippled project was invading the perceived turf of another group or individual. Invisible to the naked eye, they started erecting walls to prevent progress and keep the project from invading their department, area of expertise, whatever. The invisible wall game can keep a naïve project manager around like a rat in a maze with no way out.

The territorial strategy of invisible walls is one of the most covert strategies identified in the research. Turf mongers who find intimidation a distasteful strategy may find invisible walls more to their liking. It is a more passively aggressive game, a more "civilized" way to play out the primitive territorial drive. The game is played by carefully orchestrating rules, procedures, information access requirements, timing issues, and so on to be as inconvenient and disadvantageous for the perceived turf-invading project as possible.

Gary, the Apex sales manager mentioned in Chapter 1, is an excellent example of the invisible wall game. The implementation of the "enemy's" tracking system was effectively blocked by ensuring that training was too short and held in a distracting environment. Holding the informational meetings at 6:30 A.M. didn't help much either. Without ever appearing to publicly oppose another's efforts, the invisible wall game has killed many a project.

Malicious Obedience

The invisible wall game works best when the game player can maintain the appearance of sincere effort. It is a sleight-of-hand game. Invisible wall game players always profess to support the people they intend to disable. Our trick is to obey every request with such excruciating exactness that the obedience itself becomes an obstacle. Asked to be more careful, a software engineer can be so careful that nothing gets completed on time. A new quality initiative that invades the production engineers' authority territory can be implemented with such hypervigilance that half the factory is ready to strike in just a week. The production engineers simply salute and click their heels every time the brass walks by. The quality initiative dies an unnatural death, and, as long as no one admits anything, the quality guys may not even know they have just lost a turf war.

Even bystanders unwittingly contribute to the secrecy. To call the game for what it is would be to choose sides, and most people would rather not get involved (or are secretly pulling for the game player's side anyway). It is easier to look the other way than to interfere in a territorial game like invisible walls. To interfere is to risk being labeled an "enemy ally."

In a recent reengineering effort, Holly, a long-serving sales manager, lost part of her responsibilities to Hank, a younger "rookie" from a merged company. After three months, Hank was not performing up to standard. Since he had an exemplary track record, the obvious question was why. The answer to that question was impossible to prove, but everyone involved could see an invisible wall game being played by Holly. She selectively performed her tasks and neglected to perform specific tasks that might contribute in some way to Hank's performance. She knew certain reports would be useful to Hank, but she allowed months to slip by without generating them.

When asked why she did not perform these other tasks, Holly reportedly replied, "He never asked. . . . I'll wait until Hank tells me what he wants me to do." In this case she was being so obedient that every request was delivered and when nothing was requested, that was delivered as well. Astute territorial game players can obey every letter of the law and still wreak havoc among their perceived enemies.

Using a barely subtle display of false modesty, Holly had turned playing dumb into a very effective invisible wall. Instead of answering questions from co-workers, she would direct questions about Hank's new project to Hank. Even though she could have answered the questions herself, the delay achieved her intended result—stalling progress on the project.

Malicious obedience is not always this obvious. The examples used here are extreme only to demonstrate the game. It is highly probable that you have been on the receiving end of such games without knowing it. Let's just hope that you aren't one of those who puff up with pride at the sight of such "conscientious" employees.

Invisible walls stall, impede, block, or delay from a "behind the scenes" vantage point that is difficult to isolate. The rationalizations to obscure the true intent are frequently good enough to fool the territorial player herself! Remember, the territorial drive is a primitive drive that can be as unavailable to our awareness as the sex drive. If someone can convince himself that he buys a porn magazine for the articles, then he can convince himself that it is only in the interests of accuracy that another two weeks be spent analyzing sales figures before they are released to "those jerks in marketing."

Is There a Problem Here?

This is subtle stuff. Often enough, a simple denial will make an obstacle invisible. In the case below, a consultant found himself abruptly excluded from work that he had been doing for years.

Even if he couldn't see the wall that the new director had constructed around his decision-making territory, he could feel its
effect. It was a wall high enough and wide enough to keep him
out for good:

> *"He would always say, 'OK, the next time we need some new
> people we will call you.' Some six months would pass and I
> was never called. This went on for a while. I kept coming
> back. Face-to-face, he's agreeing. He's not giving me any in-
> dication that he doesn't want me to do it. But it never hap-
> pened. He just never followed through."*

Every time the consultant tried to call attention to the invisible wall, he was assured that it wasn't there. The conversation
would bounce off the denial and loop back to "I'll call you,"
"OK, thanks," and then "Good-bye." The game was never acknowledged, never discussed. Any attempt to address it caught
the consultant in a revolving-door conversation that ejected him
right back outside, wondering what the problem was. When it
comes down to their word against yours, they win, you lose.
And you risk being labeled an accuser. You might as well try to
show your boss your invisible friend as an invisible wall. Justifications and rationalizations make walls invisible.

The next example could easily be rationalized by this group
of individuals, who swear that there was no other time they
could meet. This tactic works particularly well, since it also creates the impression that *someone* isn't as dedicated as the rest of
the group. It is a double whammy, using both the invisible wall
game and the discredit game (Chapter 10).

> *"When they set meetings up at 7 o'clock in the morning,
> none of those people have to drop off children and get them
> to day care. I've sent them countless notes saying, 'You
> know, guys, this is my schedule,' but they just exclude me.
> They know I can't attend a 7 A.M. meeting, but they still
> have those meetings. . . . I know that they are aware of that.
> They know I can't attend."*

Do they do it *on purpose?* Not necessarily; they may be unaware of their territorial drives. Is it a territorial game? Abso-

lutely. This sort of example was given by many women who were fighting territorial games along the boundaries drawn between the sexes. Discrimination of any kind depends on covert territorial games like this one. Invisible walls, glass ceilings, and other concealed obstacles succeed in discriminating against people because they are hidden behind a cover of cooperative appearances.

Inconvenient timing, extra work, and one more "tiny" precondition selectively chosen to hit someone right where it hurts most are all examples of the invisible wall game. Territorial players can zero in on the Achilles heel of a perceived invader and bring that person down with a minimum of effort. The trick for the territorial player is to place a demand on the weakness that, to the outside world, seems like a very reasonable request.

It's even better if they can pretend that someone else is forcing them to do it.

They Won't Let Me Cooperate

One "sudden death" invisible wall strategy is to refer the issue to an unreachable, absent, higher authority. Some version of "I'd love to, but I can't" will erect an invisible wall that effectively absolves the game player of any accountability for the obstacle. Salespeople run into this all the time. A salesperson who spends time selling someone who isn't a decision maker wastes valuable time. In a territorial game, deferring to a higher authority is more of a ploy to create an invisible wall. As with the sales situation, the game can steal valuable time and yet the player can come out smelling like a rose.

> *"It looks like agreement at the time and then things get overruled. Or the guy in the meeting will say, 'That makes perfectly good sense, but I have to take it back to my management.' Then it comes back, 'No way.' They blame others."*

The time that passed while everything looked fine for the project turns into time wasted once the decision is reversed. If a negative decision had been made clear earlier, other options could have been pursued. But once that time is lost, it is lost forever.

The invisible wall game is a game of timing. As timing becomes more critical, the game becomes more destructive. A false negative can use timing to create an invisible wall, too. Sometimes a game player will say no just long enough to cheat a perceived invader of sufficient time to complete the task. By the time the decision is overturned, the opportunity is lost. The "yes" comes too late. The game player may even commiserate about "those idiots in the head office" to further enhance his image of cooperativeness.

What a perfect way to keep someone out without taking the heat! We learned this one early, probably in grammar school. If you didn't want to do something, saying "Mom says I can't" was easier than "I don't want to." Deferring to a higher authority is a great way to play a game and cover up at the same time.

Invisible resistance can occur in many forms. Distinguishing between legitimate obstacles and an invisible wall requires more information than is usually available. Part of the game is that you will never have access to the information you need to be sure. The invisible wall builder usually believes her own justifications. She isn't going to help you. Particularly if she suspects herself of territorial motives, she is unlikely to reveal those motives to others. And besides, territoriality is a purely contextual concept. It depends on your perspective as to whether that invisible wall is saving the company millions or costing it millions. The loser in a territorial game has a very difficult time proving that he or she was blocked by invisible walls.

My, My, Aren't We Upset!

Regardless of the type of wall, it is most effective when it is invisible to the objective observer. Victims of this game frequently accuse invisible wall players of being misleading—or worse. Once the effects of an invisible wall are felt there can be bad feelings all around. And since those bad feelings can't be discussed—since they are based on invisible wrongs—the buildup of frustration can erupt randomly and destructively. See if you can detect a note of bitterness in the descriptions below.

When one department publicly said it would share its physical facilities, it used invisible walls to avoid too much sharing.

"There are certain people who will say you can call them, but you might as well not call so-and-so because you know they will not share their room . . . which isn't really their room, anyway."

Here's another familiar-sounding situation:

"He would use the bureaucracy. He would tie things up in bureaucracy. He knew how to make moves and grab what he wanted and then tie it up in bureaucracy so you couldn't get it back. He would use the system. . . . He would mislead people into thinking that he was being cooperative while he was doing this other stuff behind the scenes. He always put on the face of a very cooperative person, but he was a back stabber."

They are starting to sound a bit whiny, aren't they? This is a primary source of cover-up for the invisible wall game. The obstacles tend to be small enough or reasonable enough that complaining sounds petty. If a territorial player can succeed in goading the victim to complain, it can even help the case of the game player. The complainer sounds like a wimp or may even sound paranoid. Complaining about an invisible wall rarely generates sympathy, because no one else sees it. So victims tend to keep quiet.

The frustration of keeping quiet usually fuels an escalation in the territorial battle. Even those with low territorial drives will start to feel a battle coming on when invisible walls are impeding their progress. Those who choose to endure the game in silence usually also choose to get even. In a short period of time, everyone is playing a territorial game that has precious little to do with the organization's goals.

Magic Tricks

Invisible walls depend on "magic"—smoke, mirrors, and other illusions—to stay invisible. This is one aspect of territorial games that "drives people crazy." You know the wall is there, but you can't prove it. Every time you try to articulate the obstacle, it disappears. It disappears because it sounds so petty in the retelling. "He said I could use the spare laptops, but he didn't clear it with his boss, and at the last minute his boss said no." This is unlikely to generate a chorus of "Oh, you poor thing, you."

People describing the invisible walls that thwart their initiatives, projects, and simplest tasks will display, along with the outrage, a small sense of wonder as they ask themselves, "How did they do that?" It was magic. And magic works just the same in territorial games as it works in David Copperfield's magic show.

Magic depends on speed and agility. Agility diverts attention away from the trick long enough to protect it from inspection. Speed keeps changing "the facts" quickly enough to defy analysis. The magic of the invisible wall game invites many creative applications. A wall can appear as a delayed travel approval, misplaced blueprints, or even a third dead grandmother.

In this next example, an interviewee describes a situation in which he was convinced that he was dealing with counterproductive territoriality. He couldn't prove it, but knew it was there. The magic used to hide this territorial game depended on providing reams and reams of "helpful" information to contribute to the proposed program. Stacks of printouts and reports and hours of overhead presentations mysteriously appeared.

> *"[They] completely disallowed any useful information to come out for me to take back and use as a program. The people in that meeting, therefore, accomplished not allowing the program to be started."*

What was he supposed to accuse them of, helping him to death? The most frustrating part of dealing with an invisible wall strategy is the fact that it is invisible. No discussion is possible, because there is no wall (that you can see).

Being the object of an invisible wall game is like being trapped in a Laurel and Hardy movie. You are Laurel, and every time you can convince Hardy to turn around to look at the problem, it disappears. Often, the invisible wall can be erected just long enough to be effective and then removed. Timing is critical to the "invisibleness" of invisible walls. In a "now you see it, now you don't" tactic, the territorial player can create the illusion that there is no obstruction by removing the evidence whenever anyone is looking. The boss walks in and "poof!" the obstacle is gone.

> *"This guy is practically shoving me out of his office when his boss comes in, and all of a sudden, he's all smiles and sweetness."*

The game wouldn't work if it wasn't invisible. Our corporate norms play right into the game. If you can't be a team player, then you must *look* like a team player. Image and perceptions are the arena of illusion, and the field is left wide open for tricks and prestidigitations.

> *"The actual behavior is that when everybody's in a meeting, face to face, everyone agrees in concept. Then when it comes to application of it, they have a thousand reasons why it won't work."*

Invisible walls pop up as if by magic, diverting attention away from the issue. The magic of the territorial game keeps an intruder chasing after symptoms instead of solving the problem. It's like the groundhog game at the fair, where stuffed groundhogs randomly pop up through different holes and it is the player's task to bash their little noggins with a club. A futile game, it can still seduce you into wasting your time trying. Too many earnest employees are spending their time as productively as if they were playing the groundhog game. Understanding that it is a territorial game means you can just unplug the machine at the source instead of hacking away at invisible walls that disappear as soon as you get a good shot.

THE INVISIBLE WALL GAME SELF-TEST

Imagine that a peer whose support you desperately need has just asked you to participate in his new pet project. Even though you are up to your eyeballs in other obligations, you say, "Sure." He explains that his son has just joined a pyramid scheme and he wants to give everyone in your department an opportunity to hear the two-hour presentation scheduled at a local hotel next Thursday. Your job is to send a memo to everyone and then phone to confirm their participation. Pretend that you need this guy so badly that you agreed to do this for him. List below the invisible walls that you might construct to slow down the implementation of this bizarre pet project.

1. _____

2. _____

3. _____

4. _____

5. _____

Now consider each of these and then ask yourself, "Where else have I constructed invisible walls like these?" What project or person were you trying to slow down? Try to find an example for at least three of the five tactics.

1. _____

2. _____

3. _____

4. _____

5. _____

9

The Strategic Noncompliance Game

Oops . . . Sorry.

"Oops, . . .
"did I say I would have that report to you by Friday?
"did we neglect to collect all the data you said you needed?
"did I send that bid without consulting you?
"did I say I would be there at 4:00?
"Sorry, I forgot . . . or something came up . . . or . . ."

A highly effective territorial game is to agree up front to cooperate, lull the perceived turf invader into a sense of false security, and default on the agreement at the last minute. Strategic noncompliance is a nice way of describing a behavior commonly referred to as lying. The problem with calling it the "lying game" is that no one will admit to doing it. And everybody does it at one time or another. Like all the other territorial games, it can be appropriate at times. In a legitimate battle over territory, conflict can be appropriately delayed using strategic noncompliance.

The problem with strategic noncompliance is that it can become a habit and at that point it is a mindless game. It doesn't take much to desensitize yourself to the practice of saying you will do things that you have no intention of doing. When that happens, you will tend unconsciously to turn to the strategic noncompliance game whenever you feel the slightest twinge of encroachment on your turf.

Lying is considered to be a conscious decision. More often than not, strategic noncompliance is an unconscious reflex. There are far fewer overt decisions to play this game than you might expect.

The Anatomy of Noncompliance

Strategic noncompliance game players come in two flavors: those who know very well what they are doing, and those who don't have a clue. The ones who don't have a clue vastly out- number the ones who do. They genuinely *believe* that they forgot to do what they said they would do. Or they've made up good reasons why they couldn't follow through. Again, understand- ing the rationalizations is as important as understanding the game. Most strategic noncompliance players, regardless of your belief that they "know damn well what they are doing," don't.

The common thread is that the territorial player will agree to do something when face-to-face with you and then do some- thing entirely different later on. Usually that "something en- tirely different" is inaction (or a contrary action) that is highly protective of the player's perceived territory and frequently irre- versible by the time it comes to light. While this strategy could technically fall into the "invisible walls" category, it occurs fre- quently enough to be considered a distinct territorial strategy. Strategic noncompliance deals specifically with unkept agree- ments.

As with the others, the territorial advantage of this game is one of timing. The strategic noncompliance game cheats a per- ceived invader of the opportunity to take corrective action. Since any project of importance will require the cooperation of many people, agreements are the focus of a project's progress. Once an agreement is made, effort is diverted to the next agreement. Noncompliance with a critical agreement can go undetected and unaddressed long enough to completely sabotage an initiative or project, as in the following situation:

"So they would say they were going to do something and then not do it. The effect of that was that I didn't get the

information that I needed to resolve the problem. I didn't know until it was too late."

Or this one:

"They drag their feet by saying they will run a test and then they won't run the test. Some other important priority came up and they couldn't get on the stand. For months and months they would never get the data."

As with most strategies, it is difficult to prove strategic noncompliance. Any attempt to point it out is invariably explained away. It was just an unintentional oversight, an unavoidable complication, or sheer forgetfulness. Regardless of the rationalized "disguise," this is a very common territorial strategy that relies on the appearance of cooperation and compliance, with a project or initiative, just long enough for the actual noncompliance to protect the valued territory. Noncompliance players can protect their budgets, pet projects, and very often their ability to play outside the rules. This last one is usually the territory of a seasoned old-timer who knows the ropes. Several times I've seen new managers puff up with self-satisfaction at how "easy" it was to get agreement to a new program or procedure only to find later on the old-timer still doing exactly as he pleased, well outside the new system, and completely unrepentant.

Conscious Players

The Gotcha! Game

Most of us have at least one friend who will offer a hand to be shaken or raise a hand in a high-five gesture only to remove it at the last moment, shouting "psyche!" or "gotcha!" as you stand there fooled and feeling foolish. These guys take pride in having "sucked you in" to the illusion. For some people the strategic noncompliance game is just as much fun. There are too many game players who get their jollies from playing this game to mention them separately.

Some interviewees gleefully described giving a straight-faced promise to cooperate in a project so as to lull the perceived territorial invader into a false sense of security, all the while knowing they would never comply. They knew that compliance meant sacrificing some piece of perceived territory or territorial advantage, and they wanted to keep what they had—without looking greedy, of course. For years they have survived using an "all's fair in love and war" justification system and this behavior doesn't cause them to blink an eye. The game is deeply woven into their automatic behavior patterns. Appealing to their conscience is futile as long as their internal justification system says it's OK. They will simply agree never to do it again, and then strategically choose not to comply with that agreement either.

One large company included in the research was filled with this sort of gleefully aware noncompliance players. In a group meeting of all the subsidiary companies, the chief executives of each company adamantly and fervently agreed to the CEO's demand that they equitably share resources and opportunities among the five operating units. They almost competed for the most gung-ho award. At the meeting,

> *"You get all five divisions together, they promise to work together, and they act like the CEO calls the shots. They all walk out of the room in complete agreement with him collectively. They pretend and go along with it."*

And then,

> *"They just say one thing and do something else. . . . When they go back to their five regions, it'll be the hell with everybody else."*

These guys actually enjoy the game. They get together, drink scotch, and compare notes on who pulled the best fast one on the head office or on each other. Big-ticket, highly competitive industries seem to have more than their fair share of strategic noncompliance players. In these aggressive cultures, the glorification of the rugged individualist simultaneously glorifies "whatever it takes" behaviors like strategic noncompliance.

This level of player has a certain disdain for the honest joe who wants to discuss things up front. Honest joes are labeled naïve and excluded from the inner circle for security reasons. We will explore solutions later, but it is important to note here that the gotcha player is not about to give up this game easily. It is fun for him or her. It is a habit. And it works. Any solution must offer advantages above and beyond these perceived benefits.

The Silent Veto

The other strategic noncompliance player who is actually aware of her behavior is the individual who is so self-righteous that she completely excuses her subterfuge. This person has a picture of her own territory over which flies a big I AM/WE ARE RIGHT! flag. Everyone else is labeled "Wrong!" and therefore deserves what they get. These players will protect themselves and their jobs by making public agreements with whatever company policy dictates. But when the implementation part of the agreement comes due, they hold their own version of a sit-down strike. Many reorganizations have been sabotaged by this kind of tactic. The slang term that has emerged to describe this behavior is the *silent veto*. Unwilling, or afraid, to say no in public, the game player can cast a silent veto at implementation time.

In the next example, a manager participated in a decision to reorganize in a way that would split his previous domain into two departments.

> *"One person perceived that he was going to lose a lot of power by the reorganization, so he subtly and passively resisted the whole process. He designed job responsibilities so that they crossed the boundaries that the separation was attempting to create. In meetings he would agree in concept but then would operationalize to fit the old structure. He created subrules that effectively worked against what he professed to be in compliance with."*

Granted, this sort of behavior eventually got him fired, two years later. Because the noncompliance was covert, it took a year to discover. Another year was spent "fixing" the symptoms. Meanwhile, the player's intent never wavered. His silent veto prevented progress. How much damage did the game do in those two years?

Cat Herding

The strategic noncompliance game is well suited to small agreements that can break the momentum of an initiative without generating too much attention. Resistance is better hidden in the details. As in the invisible wall game, the trick is for the territorial player to make it look as if the noncompliance is out of her hands, that her intention was to comply but that outside events or unavoidable complications or human error intervened and prevented her from doing so. Many examples were given of meetings having been arranged and then canceled at the last moment. Half an hour before the meeting seems to be the favored cancellation time. The other method is to come to the meeting and then have to rush off ("Oops, sorry, gotta get to the airport!") right before the decision needs to be made or the information is to be shared or the implementation plan starts to get some teeth.

Anyone faced with trying to arrange a meeting of individuals threatened with losing some of their valuable territory will find the job about as easy as herding a bunch of cats. In the situation below, the guy trying to get people together probably would have had more luck with the cats. This production engineer wanted to find a way to make one drive shaft that would suit each of three internal customers. He was currently spending a lot of time and effort creating three marginally different versions of the same thing. Design specifications were so close that a little cooperation would have gone a long way and saved the company a lot of money.

> "What I try to do is get all three of them in a room and see if we can't come up with something that will work for all of them. But they're very reluctant to enter into that kind of discussion. They avoid coming into the room together. They just won't schedule a meeting. If they do schedule it, then they'll call and tell me they can't make it—a half hour before the meeting they'll call and say they got called by their boss and they can't make the meeting. They do it all the time. So

they avoid the discussion as long as possible . . . or forever, if they can get away with it."

And they can get away with it. No one could accuse them of not wanting to consolidate on the design; it's just that they couldn't make the meeting. Challenging their excuses would only generate antagonism. As long as they want to avoid that meeting they will always find ways to avoid it.

Unconscious Players

Being Behind It 100 Percent

Most people caught up in the game of strategic noncompliance are blissfully unaware that they are playing a game. They've said they are on the bandwagon so often that they really believe it. They don't want to be killjoys. Maybe they got caught up in the moment; maybe an overzealous team member badgered them into saying yes. Who knows? But in the beginning, they are "behind it 100 percent" and "you can count on" them.

> *"He wasn't aggressive with it. He was passive. He didn't say, 'This thing is not going to work.' He said, 'This will work; I'm all for it; we have to do it; we have to make sure it's successful; I want to make sure it's successful. . . . Just let me train these people and when they are ready to go, then we'll move along to the next step.' So he agreed in principle but yet his behavior was that he delayed it as long as possible."*

Unconscious strategic noncompliance players are usually more sensitive to the social implications of noncompliance. In order to avoid the bad feelings of saying no, they say yes. They feel better and the up-front agreement protects their good reputation as cooperative team players.

> *"There was clearly one executive who would 'roger up' on everything but then do his own thing. He would agree on the*

*way things would be done in a meeting and then go out and
do as he damn well pleased."*

Unconscious strategic noncompliance players may initially
have every intention of following through on their promises.
More than likely, they have severely underestimated the costs in
terms of their personal territory. Sharing staff sounds reasonable
in a meeting, but finding someone else to do the work is something else entirely.

*"They just wouldn't release the people. Not all of them. Some
did and some didn't. The ones that didn't—they had agreed
in the meeting, but when it came down to it, two weeks later,
they didn't."*

It is a good idea to monitor the ones who are "behind it 100
percent." These gung-ho team players may not have considered
the implications of their promises or could be operating on the
theory that it is easier to ask forgiveness than permission.

Did I Say That?

Strategic noncompliance players can stay unaware of their game
in different ways. Territorial impulses are so unattractive to us
that we make up rationalizations that even *we* believe. More objective observers can see right through them, but we don't. Many
of the interviewees described situations in which it was obvious
that the interviewee did not believe the strategic noncomplier
was aware of his "true motivations" (protecting territory). Obviously there is no way to prove true motivations, and pointing
them out is impolite.

*"That's part of the politeness—the spur of the moment
agreeing to it. But when you start going back into your den
and realizing the point that you were coerced into considering, the ground that perhaps you gave up, you reconsider it
and muster yourself again on some other resources and decide 'I'm back to my original position.' . . . [It] happens all
the time in Congress."*

This flip-flopping demonstrates how a situation can be completely altered into a territorial battle. In a larger group, the big picture reframes a sacrifice as "good" for the group. But its being "bad" for a subgroup is often more important for an individual. Too many times the resulting inner conflict corrupts the agreements originally made in good faith.

> *"They go back and they say they never said it or they say they didn't agree to it. They deny it. Later on down the line, they deny having made agreements. I don't know if it's because they're afraid or what. I don't know what their reasoning is."*

They probably don't have any reasoning. Humans are not known for being especially vigilant in examining all their incongruities. When faced with contradictions between what we say and what we do, we would usually rather talk about something else.

You Will Never Know for Sure

To be successful, the game of strategic noncompliance depends on a good excuse. Excuses are tricky. In school, there probably was one unfortunate individual whose dog really did eat his homework. However, most excuses are just that—excuses. Distinguishing between legitimate excuses and bald-faced lies means understanding that they are two ends of a continuum that has no distinct crossover point. Even if you can make the distinction, it isn't much help. In organizational turf wars there is little advantage to seeing the excuse for what it is. Calling a co-worker a liar is not on the list of top ten methods for increasing cooperation.

Excuses demand the benefit of the doubt. To disbelieve an excuse is to draw a more distinct territorial line separating two groups or two individuals. Most of those interviewed never called a territorial player on the game of strategic noncompliance.

> *"He came back to me and claimed that he absolutely forgot that we agreed that we'd get back together before any action*

*was taken. So I had no choice but to say I believed him if that
is what he is telling me."*

*"If we were to tell them this [that they were not complying],
they would claim that they had some other reason for doing
it."*

Accusations may be an impulsive reaction to the game of
strategic noncompliance, but it was usually an impulsive reaction that started the turf war. Another impulsive reaction only
escalates the battle. Strategic noncompliance can only be con-
trolled from inside each individual. Attributing malicious intentions to the actions of others just makes things worse. It is much
better to realize that you will never know for sure whether the
strategic noncompliance was intended or not—if only because
the game player may never know for sure either. Accusing someone of lying is just attacking a symptom instead of dealing with
the root cause of the problem.

Whether conscious or not, the strategy of noncompliance is
a very effective and frequently used covert territorial game. Its
effectiveness depends on plausible rationalization and timing. It
is almost impossible to prove and equally difficult to avoid since
it is only apparent after the fact. The most significant impact on
organizations is the distrust that this game breeds. All the games
breed distrust, but strategic noncompliance is particularly lethal
to the cooperative spirit that moves an organization forward.

THE STRATEGIC NONCOMPLIANCE
GAME SELF-TEST

You treat different people differently. That is normal. You have varying levels of trust with everyone you work with. Consider the categories in the table below that break down your standards of agreement into four different levels. Without too much thinking, write the names of at least two people in each category. Be honest. If you need to, write the names lightly in pencil and then erase them.

I always keep agreements with these people.	*I have been known to break agreements with these people.*	*I usually tell these people what they want to hear.*	*I let these people believe that I agree with them for as long as possible.*
1. _____	1. _____	1. _____	1. _____
2. _____	2. _____	2. _____	2. _____
3. _____	3. _____	3. _____	3. _____
4. _____	4. _____	4. _____	4. _____

Look at the people you listed in the right-hand columns. In the space below, write down the threat that each may represent to your turf. What territory of yours (specifically) might they be threatening? Is it information, relationships, your decision-making authority, or some aspect of your own self-image (your progress, your status)?

Name	*Threat Posed*
1. _____	_____
2. _____	_____
3. _____	_____
4. _____	_____

Choose one person you could move from the columns on the right to one of those on the left. What would thereby change in your relationship? What would be the benefit to the organization?

Name	Change in Relationship	Benefit to Organization

What would be the downside? Is there a way to protect yourself against that downside?

_____

_____

_____

_____

_____

10

The Discredit Game

He's OK, but I wouldn't trust him.

Acquiring, maintaining, and protecting territory requires power. There is a lot of power in credibility. The more credible the speaker, the more power he or she has to influence co-workers, subordinates, and superiors. To be credible is, in a sense, to have a cooperation credit account to draw upon when needed. Two people can say the same thing and get totally different reactions depending on how much credibility the group assigns each of them. If a mailboy points out a new product opportunity, no one listens. If the CEO points one out, executives will fall all over themselves to agree and to be the first *to act* on that statement. Credibility has the power to create action—the sort of action that is important to a territorial player. Therefore, decreasing the amount of credibility that a perceived territorial opponent carries is an effective strategy in protecting turf. It diminishes that person's ability to create action. It strips him of power.

Once it becomes a game, discrediting can hide behind a variety of rationalizations. A common rationalization is "I was only telling the truth." The fact that a discrediting comment or innuendo is true does not preclude it from being a game. The truth can be selectively presented in order to create a discrediting effect. Even Mother Teresa can look bad when the truth is selectively reported. Another rationalization used frequently appeals to the fears of those involved. Explanations such as "I was just trying to help you" are often used by game players to excuse themselves from taking responsibility for indulging in a bit of character assassination.

The sales staff described below had rationalized their disparaging remarks about "those turkeys in Columbia" by focusing on serving the customer. In the name of reliable service, they have used the discredit game to steal territory away from this sister office. The game may have started as a solution for poor service, but it escalated into the discrediting game pretty quickly.

> *"Obviously, our salespeople have given our customers that message, 'You can count on us, but those turkeys in Columbia you can't count on.' They enhance their status, or they push off the problems. They don't take responsibility for the problems by laying it on another location. And now that location has a bad rep with our customer."*

Inflicting credibility flesh wounds not only reduces the power of the perceived invaders but can fuzz up their thinking with anger or fear so that they become less clearheaded in defending themselves. This game works on two levels. On the surface, discrediting will decrease the power wielded by an individual's opinions, informal authority, or influence. The ultimate objective is to tarnish the perceived quality of an individual's (or group's) logic, clarity, analytical ability, or competence—in other words, to get as many important people as possible to think that the guy or group is stupid, careless, or something equally demeaning.

At the second level, the discredit game can goad an otherwise rational human being to "lose it" and thus lose valuable credibility. Being the object of constant criticism or a clandestine smear campaign can give even a calm, tolerant person a bad attitude. For some discredit game players, the resulting emotional outburst (or shutdown) of their victim can do more damage to an "enemy's" credibility than any amount of external discrediting can. One common discredit sequence that can operate on both levels is the "setup."

The Setup

The setup is an old trick that allows the discredit player to discredit another person and at the same time avoid any appearance of criticizing. In fact, done properly, the discrediter can even appear to be trying to help. This can be accomplished in a variety of ways. Some interviewees described a setup routine in which a territorial player purposefully asks a co-worker a question to which the unfortunate person is certain not to know the answer. As the co-worker fumbles around with the difficult question, his credibility steadily declines. An exaggerated attempt to cover for him further diminishes his credibility. The casual observer, seeing this lack of knowledge, is tempted to wonder about other issues that might prompt a similar fumbling and bumbling. The setup usually begins with a question the inquirer already knows how to answer:

> *"I have seen a person ask a question that he's perfectly capable of answering [for himself] and then two of them would quickly turn their heads toward the mark and stare as if he should know the answer. They are purposely putting him in the position of saying he doesn't know."*

Another setup routine involves an impromptu interrogation that continues until a weak link is discovered. If the discrediter can fluster the target of the game, then a good idea can deteriorate into appearing to be a rash, even dangerous assumption that could have cost the company big bucks if the game player hadn't intervened. In this form of the setup, the game player gets to be a hero into the bargain:

> *"The way he would do that would be that even though it was a brainstorming strategy session, he would bore in with 'What's the basis for that?' 'What's your factual data?' Now it was very obvious that he wouldn't do that with everybody. He would accept some ideas without the factual basis. Somehow for some reason, X would have to have a whole list of things—and they were never good enough."*

If you pay attention, you will find that questions are not always questions. Sometimes questions are really statements, like "Are you really going to do *that*?" and sometimes they are attacks, like "How will you compensate for the outrageous expense?" In the setup version of the discredit game, questions can do a lot of damage—and protect a lot of turf.

One interesting thing to note about this game is that the discrediting statement need not be directly related to any relevant competence.

His Mother Wears Army Boots, You Know

Human beings tend to generalize and will make global assumptions based on a very small piece of data. Our brains are designed to jump to conclusions when a warning is involved. Originally, this saved our lives. A rustle in the bamboo might prompt a "don't go there" response that crossed over to all bamboo thickets. Our brains are just trying to keep us safe, and back then a little overcompensation wasn't a problem. Today, however, a single piece of negative information should not be enough to write off another person. Yet it often is—even when it's a piece of information completely unrelated to any relevant competence.

A territorial player may casually mention that a co-worker belongs to an Elvis fan club, subscribes to a UFO magazine, or wore two mismatched shoes. None of which has anything to do with this person's ability to administer a budget. Such a comment can still generate the desired raised eyebrows and giggles. The consequent removal of this individual from a task force controlling the "casual" conversationalist's budget is sure to be "well justified" but subtly traceable to the "UFO thing." The individual may never know that she was the target of the discredit game. She will probably be more curious about how the game player managed to double his resource budget.

As in the rest of these covert games, no one would be caught dead doing this in an obvious manner. The more finesse that is used in causing important people to question another's credibility, the more effective this strategy can be. Consider the following description, in which a territorial player would

> *"question in a nice way the reliability of someone who has had a drinking problem. In a meeting—and I'm sure individually with the boss—he was seeking to discredit this person in the nicest possible way."*

No words need be spoken to create the desired effect. Non-verbal discredits can be communicated through a well-placed look of surprise, a tilt of the head and a little grunt, or an exaggerated leaning back combined with a deep sigh. Frequently, the discredit game need only cast doubt on a person's ability in order to protect territory. Because the fast pace of our world requires instantaneous decisions, discrediting is becoming a more destructive game.

The Comic Kill

It seems that territorial players are always looking for a tasteful way to go about character assassination. If they want to discredit people in the "nicest possible way," then humor can be a good disguise. Like the sarcasm used in the intimidation game, humor is readily defended with a quick "just kidding."

> *"He would sometimes use humor to put him down. He'd make comments like 'Well, let's stay strategic here,' and that implies that the comment was something less than strategic. We'd laugh, but, you know, they were direct put-downs."*

Funny put-downs can pack a double punch to a person's credibility: first, the implied put-down; then, the revelation of an apparent lack of a sense of humor when the attacked one doesn't laugh. (Most successful executives have trained themselves to guffaw at the time, relying on getting even later.) Again, there is great difficulty in distinguishing between innocent teasing and purposeful discrediting. Like the other games, it relies on being covert and can easily disguise itself as innocent humor.

The game player may not even know it is a game. A wonderful sense of humor is a gift to be admired. Those overgenerously endowed may get caught up in the admiration they inspire in others. They may be totally unaware of the territorial impulses that lead them to select the butt of their jokes, particularly when the targets appear to be chosen on the basis of their ethnicity or sex. There are a few ex-Texaco executives who learned this the hard way.

Discriminating Remarks

One particularly insidious way to discredit another individual is
to appeal to the latent prejudices that burden most human beings. Few people grew up without learning some form of prejudice. If only to reduce the amount of data to be processed, the
brain will look for reasons to write off entire categories of people, places, or things. The current pressures to hide prejudice
only drive the prejudice deeper into a variety of covert behaviors. Hidden behind covert games, prejudice does even more
damage.

When prejudice already exists, a territorial player can discredit an individual merely by activating the fears associated
with a particular prejudice. In the following example, hecklers
in a predominantly American audience effectively discredited a
speaker with stage whispers of ridicule and attacks on the
speaker's ethnicity.

> *"This is a big group meeting . . . people German, British, or
> of other European descent speaking. People were just harass-
> ing them completely. They would say, 'Why do we have to
> listen to this?' They used names like Krauts, Frogs, etc., for
> whomever. They were swearing. . . . The effect was that they
> didn't listen to what the person was saying. They distracted
> people that were probably listening and not behaving like
> that. Whether they agreed with everything they said I don't
> know. But they were certainly moving with them. They effec-
> tively cut off anyone's ability to receive whatever data was
> coming from these Europeans. They pulled in anyone within
> earshot from listening to whatever was happening. They
> brought in people who typically might have listened, but who
> might now have those viewpoints."*

Appealing to prejudice as a discrediting strategy taps a
deeply placed, usually emotional reaction that can be very powerful in protecting territory. Prejudice is based on fear and fear is
a strong motivator. It is also a stealthy motivator. Fear, activated
through prejudice, can drive behavior for a long time before
quiet reflection may highlight the injustice. By the time a group
considers the consequences of a casually slanderous comment
like "bunch of black jelly beans," the damage is done. Tragically,

most prejudice-based discrediting is never exposed to the restraining effect of self-reflection. It simply solidifies divisions and perceptions of "us" and "them," for both us and them—whoever they may be.

Fear can also be invoked by creating perceptions of a specific threat. Labeling anyone as a risk effectively excludes them from valued territory.

Rivalry in the Helping Professions

Appealing to self-interest boosts the effectiveness of a discrediting strategy. If a game player can construct a dangerous-enough scenario, others will begin to associate the target with danger. Even a nagging doubt can be enough to kill another's chances at coveted territory.

Consider again the broad territorial battle between the fields of psychology and psychiatry. The territory in this case concerns the legislated right to prescribe medication. Psychiatrists have it and psychologists want it. In this interview with a psychologist, it is clear he believed that the psychologists who wanted the right to prescribe

> *"were being labeled by the psychiatrists as a public health hazard . . . doing a disservice or harm to the people that [were] rightfully 'ours' to serve and not yours to serve."*

Building on the implication that great harm might result if psychologists were given the right to prescribe, some psychiatrists used the discredit game.

> *"They would do things to discredit us. They would claim that not having enough knowledge . . . you [psychologists] were endangering your patient. . . . Yet they ignore the fact that 85 percent of the psychotropic medications are prescribed by nonpsychiatrically trained medical doctors."*

Did you notice that the interviewee slipped in his own shot at the psychiatrists' credibility? Of course the information is relevant. Ultimately, this argument *should* be about the patient's well-being. That doesn't mean that there isn't a game going on.

When the spirit behind the words is more concerned with winning territory than anything else, even the most legitimate-sounding concerns are subject to inspection. Games are destructive to collaborative effort. When two sides are pitted against each other in a struggle over territory, discrediting erodes trust and cooperation and can ultimately sabotage any hope of an optimal outcome.

> "It is a claim, disclaim, back-and-forth process of whose rightful territory it is. Back-and-forth arguments about the other side's experience, background, education, credentials, etc. took up a lot of time. Belittling each of these separately until the result was to discredit the whole person, the whole group, as a tactic to remove their access to patients."

It is unlikely that the patients won this one. Discrediting games can drain both sides of valuable work time. It can leave a trail of vendettas that play out over the years. It is very destructive and very covert. The game is protected by the ultimate disguise—concern for another human being's safety and well-being. This makes the discredit game very effective in protecting territory. The issue here is intent. Presenting data to protect and presenting data to discredit are different objectives. The challenge in identifying a territorial strategy is to consider the intent (whether conscious or unconscious) in presenting discrediting information.

The Outsiders

Often those perceived as a threat to established lines of territory are new employees or outside consultants. Once branded an outsider, the new employee or consultant is automatically excluded from valuable information, relationships, or influence on decisions. Why? Because they are outsiders. The concept of "outsider" is a function of territoriality; without territorial lines, that concept is meaningless. A discrediter need only perpetuate the label to activate primitive territorial behaviors that exclude and diminish the targeted individual or group.

If you agree that we have some form of territorial drive, then outsiders will automatically activate this drive. To the primitive emotional brain an outsider will either help your cause or hinder it. Discrediters jump on the chance to ensure that outsiders are perceived as the hindering kind rather than the helping kind. A casual reference can shift listeners' minds in the desired direction. "We don't really know much about him" or "How much could he possibly know about our business?" is enough to activate automatic territorial defenses.

When the outsiders themselves are not susceptible to the discredit game, then discrediting the people who brought them in is the next best thing:

> *"They would ridicule the sincerity of the fans of the new consultants. They would make them sound gullible. Saying, 'Well, that sounds pretty damn bizarre to me. What relevance does it have? You guys are turning into groupies, for God's sake.'"*

No direct criticism is necessary. It is enough to make reference to the outsider's status as an outsider. And if that isn't enough, then there is always the tactic of fueling perceptions of danger that naturally arise with change.

> *"There's a real danger we could get into groupthink here."*

Vague and easily defended, these comments can nevertheless have a negative effect on the cooperative response a work group might otherwise give to a new addition. The outsider can spend more time overcoming the label of outsider than contributing to the organization's objectives.

Territorial players who use the discredit game to protect territory or win new territory are rarely aware that they are playing a game. The emotions activated by a territorial drive will hide the game from their awareness. In their unawareness, the discredit game can turn a word of caution into a snowball of distrust that effectively immobilizes the target.

The game of discrediting can arbitrarily shift the relative weight of data, cloud the accuracy of information, and confuse the true priorities of a team. Once caught up in a tit-for-tat exchange of discrediting comments, the productivity of any work group quickly goes down the drain.

THE DISCREDIT GAME SELF-TEST

Write down the names of people in your organization who best fit the categories in the table below. Draw from your own subjective evaluations and the conversations you have heard. Again, you may want to use a pencil and then erase what you have written. For the sake of the exercise, give yourself permission to call it as you see it.

Ultimately Credible	*Good Strong Image*	*Weak, Pushover Image*	*Definitely Not to Be Trusted*	*A Putz, a Real Bozo*

Now, take one name apiece from the three right-hand categories and for each name identify at least one instance where you helped contribute to that perception or helped perpetuate that perception by your words or actions. Can you remember a story you shared, a meaningful glance, a roll of your eyes, or other discrediting action?

1. _____   _____

2. _____   _____

3. _____   _____

Beside each name, give a brief description of the turf this individual occupies that you don't, or vice versa. What is the line that divides you from these people?

1. _____   _____

2. _____   _____

3. _____   _____

How have they been discredited?

1. ———————————————————————————————

2. ———————————————————————————————

3. ———————————————————————————————

How much of that is justified?

1. ———————————————————————————————

2. ———————————————————————————————

3. ———————————————————————————————

What would happen if you took on the task of PR agent for one of these people—improving his image? (Choose the one who most deserves it.) Imagine telling stories and behaving in ways that enhance that person's image in your organization. Other than the confusion and disbelief generated by your sudden change of heart, what would be the impact on the organization? What positive outcomes might occur as a result of your actions?

———————————————————————————————

———————————————————————————————

———————————————————————————————

———————————————————————————————

———————————————————————————————

———————————————————————————————

11

The Shunning Game

The Amish solution.

As Robert Fulghum discovered, kindergarten has a lot to teach us about human behavior. Most of us learned the tactic of shunning around that time. There was one little boy or girl who would not leave you alone, who invaded your space, pulled your hair, or knocked your books out of your arms. Mother, Father, or Teacher probably gave you this little piece of advice: "Ignore him and he'll stop." And if you could make yourself do it, it worked. That's because human beings need attention. Depriving an individual of attention can have a powerfully punishing effect that can raise the stakes to a level too high for comfort. Little kids, dogs, factory workers, and CEOs can all be shunned to the point where they give up ground. Raise the psychological stakes high enough and they will back away from protected territory without realizing the emotional origins of their retreat.

Through the shunning game, the stakes can be raised just enough to justify discontinuing a project, an initiative, or an investigation that seems to be invading protected territory. Even for the thick-skinned, shunning can hurt.

Shunning began before written history. It originally functioned as a way to kill off the undesirables by not extending protection to them. In some cultures, it has been institutionalized. Cultures that are very concerned with protecting territorial boundaries, preventing infiltration, and restraining abandonment of or watering down of the group's norms are more likely to use shunning to police group members. Shunning is a traditional tactic used by the Amish, an old Pennsylvania German religious sect, to control members' behavior—and it works pretty well, too.

Anyone who seriously violates the Amish ground rules can be targeted for shunning. No one speaks to her. Her presence is not acknowledged. She is completely ignored. Family, previous friends, and acquaintances all collude to deny the offending individual the experience of acknowledgment. Psychological survival is fed by acknowledgment. Shunning strips an individual of core psychological territory: confirmation of her existence. In its extreme form, it is a brutal punishment. People have changed their minds on very important issues to avoid further shunning.

Of course, in organizations shunning is not usually taken up by the entire organization. Often there will be a certain group that targets a perceived invader for exclusion. The exclusion can be subtle or overt. However, even overt shunning will be tempered under certain conditions. Most shunning looks childish to anyone without a vested interest in the turf war. The presence of anyone outside the turf war is enough to embarrass a shunner into acting civil again, at least until he leaves.

Even if the shunned don't come around to the territorial player's way of thinking, the act of shunning can at least remove them from being a threat. Most people won't hang around where they aren't wanted. If it is their job to "hang around," shunning can be a powerful method of excluding them. Subordinates can shun a manager to the point where contact is gradually reduced to a minimum. In the following situation, a subordinate was leading the corporate equivalent of a mutiny. As he ignored his boss, others also began to ignore her, until she had to ask a question several times before she got an answer.

> *"His response when I would ask him questions was to say, 'I'm working with so-and-so on that—what do you need to know for?' AND I'M HIS MANAGER!"*

Obviously, the shunning was getting to her. It can get to just about anyone. According to the organization chart, these people worked for her. According to the turf war results, she was losing ground. If she didn't start making some territorial moves herself, they wouldn't be working for her much longer. She might withstand the emotional effects, but shunning can cut a manager off from vital information that she needs in order to do her job. You are miles away from the corporate grapevine when people are pretending you don't exist—or acting as if they wished you didn't.

Creating an Invisible Man

Shunning is a childish, primitive way of branding someone as an outsider. Unless the shunner is a person of special importance, the shunning game is more effective when played by a group. When several people begin to act as if you don't exist, you begin to wonder yourself. It is either a confidence killer or a maddening irritant. A victim may muster up a calm exterior, but shunning almost always generates an emotional reaction.

Mergers are traditional "us and them" situations. Shunning is frequently played in the early stages of a merger. In this next example, Brad, who was originally from the larger of the two merged companies, began reporting to Hector, a manager from the smaller company. Organizationally, Hector already had more power, so from a rational standpoint he would seem to have already won any relevant territorial battle. But territorial urges are not rational. It could have been a territorial case of "little big man." Hector was still identifying himself as being from the smaller company. He was operating from old drives, old emotions, and old tapes:

> *"When Brad called Hector, Hector said he 'didn't have time' to talk to him, that he would be getting around to it but it wouldn't 'be anytime soon. So don't bother me. Don't call me, I'll call you when I need to talk.' It made Brad feel like he wasn't a part of the team, and didn't want to be either."*

Shunning was Hector's limbic system response to hearing a voice from the other company. It was not a considered reaction. There was no rational thought. His emotional brain chose for him, and it chose badly. It would take months to undo the damage done in this one conversation.

Shunning doesn't have to be repeated very often. It only takes one or two times. After just this one experience of being shunned, Brad was only half as likely to call again. Our rational brains may tell us to "just ignore them," but a little humiliation goes a long way.

You're Just Being Overly Sensitive

Whether the shunning game is overt or covert, it is rarely discussed. Anyone being shunned usually feels foolish complaining that "they're ignoring me." It sounds too whiny coming from an executive. Observers usually don't point it out, since it is so easily denied as an oversight. Yet, judging from the interviews, the territorial tactic of shunning is not only frequently used but very effective. In meeting with managers from two other newly merged companies, a participant made this observation:

> *"When it would have been an appropriate time to solicit input from the other members of the team, he systematically went around the room and skipped the X Company people. It was obvious that he was going around the room and when he got to them he skipped over them. He ignored their existence. I don't know if it was done consciously. But that doesn't matter."*

No, it doesn't matter. The individuals who were passed over got the message loud and clear: Their input was not valued, they weren't welcome, and this was most definitely not their turf anymore. Imagine sitting there yourself, and don't be too quick to assume that you wouldn't just sit there either. If you were outnumbered, you'd probably sit there and take it too. Whatever you did, the experience is almost sure to escalate divisive feelings and prompt more territorial games.

Shunning is one of the psychological tactics of a territorial battle. The objective is to deliver a strong negative message that reads "We don't want you here." The executive described below was unfortunately targeted by a higher-level executive as the target of a shunning game.

"Any time that there were meetings called at the strategy level, he would either 'inadvertently' not contact the other person, or a number of them were scheduled at the exact same time as this executive's weekly staff meetings."

No one can argue with an "inadvertent" oversight. Excluding someone from a meeting doesn't always indicate shunning, but when it does, people usually know it. When the exclusion itself becomes a message, the intent is usually shunning. Except for those who truly are overly sensitive, most people know when they are being shunned. Sometimes it is their first clue that they have inadvertently trespassed onto someone's perceived territory.

Maybe It's B.O.

One interviewee described an instance in which he happily stepped up to join two other managers who were discussing weekend sailing only to find that the conversation began to fade away. There was an obvious shift in the tone of the conversation. Before he stepped up, it was animated and enthusiastic. After he joined, shorter sentences, longer pauses, and some watch checking replaced the previous liveliness. In a very short time, both the other managers were gone and the individual stood there alone, feeling very shunned.

The exclusion is invisible to the rational eye but acutely apparent to the emotional eye. One person sits down at a table full of people and in ten minutes she finds herself alone. Sure, it could be coincidence. Sometimes it is. Sometimes it isn't. The high school method of checking to see if it's coincidence or not is still used in adulthood. "What's the matter, do I have B.O. or somethin'?" will almost always create a chorus of denials. The tone of the denials, however, is a clue to the territorial intent. When a group behaves as if an individual actually *smells* bad, it is probably using the shunning game to send a territorial message.

Since avoidance is not always possible, there are other ways to play the shunning game. In the following example there was very little objective evidence to point to as shunning behavior. Yet the person interviewed got the message:

"There was a lot of whispering and things going on. I'd walk back there to hand someone something and, all of a sudden, the conversation would completely stop and the atmosphere would get very tense."

The silence can be deafening. Eyes staring straight ahead, the exchange of meaningful smirks, or huffs of disgust add to the iciness of the silence. Nonverbal communication is especially suited to shunning. Dismissive mannerisms tell the excluded whose territory they are on.

Firmly protected by being in the realm of the intangible and thus unprovable, dismissive mannerisms are secret codes to others in the room. Once addressed, a territorial player may pause momentarily before deigning to turn and give the speaker eye contact. This pause demonstrates a visible reluctance even to look at the shunned individual. An exasperated, exaggerated sigh also works. "Accidentally" forgetting someone's name or using the wrong name can create a shunning effect. Or shunning can mean simply ignoring someone's input.

"I think they shut them out of the conversation. They go right on by them."

Valid ideas presented for the group's discussion are not written on the whiteboard along with the others. Opinions and comments are ignored. The same idea offered by someone who is in the "in-group" can magically become the center of the conversation. The idea may even get extra attention to further clarify the shunning. But the target of the territorial game is still ignored and excluded, especially if he demands credit for the idea.

Of course, there is ignoring and then there is *ignoring*.

Active Ignoring

Some people like to be more obvious in their shunning strategy. This can be owing to a mean streak or it can be a public call to

arms. The more obvious the shunning game, the more it operates as a call to observers to "choose sides."

> *"There was one meeting where it really came to a head. He
> planted himself next to me, turned his back to me, and was
> encroaching on my space. . . . He came into the meeting, sat
> right next to me . . . and turned his back, totally. It was a big
> table. . . . He physically made a wall, turned his back in front
> of seven people. . . . He positioned himself between me and
> the boss and turned his back on me. That meeting lasted a
> couple of hours. He maintained that position the whole
> time."*

This was a blatant act of shunning. Staring right through
someone as if he didn't exist, turning away from an individual,
ensuring that there is no chair for someone to sit in, leaving her
off the organization chart or address list—all these tactics are
designed to actively ignore a targeted individual. When the
shunning game is this obvious, talking to the individual or acknowledging him in any way is to risk being branded as being
on "their side." Acknowledging someone is a forced choice; either you do or you don't. In a turf war, any choice will be considered a public declaration of loyalty. Immature? Sure. If
immaturity means mindlessly responding to emotional urges,
then all the territorial games are, by definition, immature.

> *"The behavior was totally ignored. There was no conversa-
> tion about the behavior. Nobody came to me. I didn't talk to
> him or anyone else about it. I just swallowed it."*

As obvious as this example was, no one discussed it. Nei-
ther the observers nor the victim of the shunning. No one. If this
person had not been interviewed, the situation would never have
seen the light of day. The cultural norms around shunning protect this territorial game from exposure. It is an "undiscussable"
topic. When it is obvious, the target is usually too embarrassed
to speak up, and observers don't speak up for fear of receiving
the same treatment. When it is not so obvious, it is too easily
denied. The shunner herself may succeed in remaining completely unaware of the behavior and its effects.

Like the other strategies, shunning can be unconscious and perceived by the shunner as "purely unintentional." The situation below is a good example of a shunning game that is played below the level of conscious awareness. Social events frequently play host to territorial skirmishes. People construct artificial divisions between the work setting and the social events that arise from it. The emotional brain doesn't make these distinctions. Being shunned from a social event will *feel* the same to the shunned individual as being shunned from a meeting. Even though it occurs in another context, a social event can operate as a battleground for an extended turf war.

> *"They exclude me from things like lunches. There was recently someone who had a baby shower for someone who just had a child—one of the men who works for me. I was not invited . . . so it's a social exclusion sometimes. That happens at lot. Golfing, tennis, other events, I'm excluded."*

And being excluded tells her something about her status in the group: They don't want her there. Something she did stepped on their turf. No matter how professional these people are, they are playing a game that will ultimately bleed off into the workplace. Unchecked, the shunning game will begin to affect decisions, limit the amount of cooperation, and filter the information flowing between the shunners and the shunned.

Paradoxically, ignoring someone is not the only way to send a message of exclusion.

Death by Politeness

Death by politeness is the Academy Award method of shunning. This method has been perfected at the highest levels of government and in many charity organizations and churches. It is also a prerequisite for any southern belle hoping to join the Junior League. It is a backwards application of the shunning game that uses excessive, highly visible acts of inclusion to exclude. It has been said that the Southerner's kiss of death is a smile accompanied by a well-placed "That's nice." Politeness is not always nice. It can even be cruel.

"They will sit one on the one side and the other on the other side. They will use incredibly—disgustingly at first— nauseatingly polite behavior to each other. . . . It is amazing, nauseating, the knife is so thick about this politeness. It is so superficial. . . . You see it on the floor of Congress when they say, 'My esteemed colleague and Senator from so and so,' when they hate his guts. You know it, but it's a sense of being a flag."

By some strange twist (common in human behavior), excessive politeness can operate as shunning behavior. The obviously forced nature of the inclusion creates a sort of behavioral sarcasm, excluding another from the inner circle. It is a Judas kiss that publicly paints the recipient of such politeness with "enemy" markings.

Protected by the guise of being politically correct, a male peer might overemphasize his use of feminine pronouns because he "doesn't want to offend Jane, here." His excessive politeness ("Any CEO . . . he—excuse me, *she*—") merely emphasizes Jane's separateness, her difference from the rest of the group. It even sends the message that Jane is "touchy" about that sort of thing, while the speaker comes off as being sensitive to her needs.

True inclusion in a group decreases formality. Excessive politeness simply communicates the fact that this level of inclusion does not exist. In a work setting, formality works as a method both of shunning and of slowing the flow of information. Shunners may choose to deliver a formal report when a "heads up" comment would have sufficed. Arranging a larger meeting than necessary or giving a visitor the grand tour when she just wanted to sit and talk will demonstrate her outsider status both to her and to anyone else observing.

Whether delivered by excessive politeness or deliberate ignoring, the message of the territorial game of shunning is "out." It can be "get out," "stay out," "you are out," or "you will soon be out." Many territorial protectionist strategies rely on shunning as a communication tool to trespassers and as a deterrent to future trespassing.

THE SHUNNING GAME SELF-TEST

Think about your peers. Who is "in"? Who is "out"?

In the space below, write the names of several people you work with in the column in which you think they belong.

Who Is "In"	Who Is "Out"

How do you tell the difference between the "ins" and the "outs"?

_____

_____

What role have you played in establishing this order? _____

_____

_____

How do you think it makes those who are "out" feel? _____

_____

_____

What effect does their "in" or "out" status have on their ability to be productive?

_____

_____

_____

12

The Camouflage Game

Look, a head in the road!

If you have ever walked into a meeting feeling focused and clear-headed and later walked out dazed and confused, then it is possible you have encountered the camouflage game. In a turf war, as in any war, camouflage is quite useful. It's unlikely that a territorial player will put on green and brown fatigues, but he will find other ways to blend with the background and otherwise confuse any objective reading of the visible terrain. Smoke and mirrors can decide critical territorial battles in an ongoing turf war.

The purpose of camouflage is to distract or confuse a perceived territorial invader long enough to defuse or deflect a territorial trespass. The simplest example of this tactic is the Three Stooges ploy of pointing and shouting "Look over there!" with enough believability that Mo swirls around and doesn't catch Larry stealing his cookie, the trumpet, or next year's budget. In meetings, the tactic operates much the same way—sending someone on a wild goose chase rather than the intended path that leads into protected territory. There are many tactics available to the camouflage game player.

The Untracker

To win a turf war, a territorial player faced with a freight train invasion need only orchestrate a small detour. If he can untrack the invaders, the territory is safe while the invaders careen help-lessly toward an unintended destination. In the camouflage game, an untracker can use the inertia behind a fast-moving agenda to turn a (perceived) invasion into a train wreck.

In the following situation, a researcher who was trying to accelerate approval on his project encountered formidable oppo-sition. Camouflaged in cooperative clothing, Hal, a self-pro-fessed "fan" of the project, helped track it right into months and months of red tape and a debilitating approval process. With "fans" like this, the project needed no enemies. Hal's skill as an "untracker" is evident in the description: "You feel comfortable going down [the primrose path] the whole way through." The mark of a successful untracker is that none of the victims know they have been untracked until it is too late.

> *"Hal was there only as a sophisticated 'untracker' in groups. [Untrackers] get you going down the primrose path. . . . You feel comfortable going down there the whole way through. What he knew [was] that if you have a bunch of fairly bright people . . . you can make it sound plausible. In order to avoid the implementation of my idea, Hal said it sounded great, he thought it had great potential, but 'we need to submit this to the Human Use Committee and get this clinical investigat-ing committee to approve the scientific merit.' And so on and so forth—taking it to the point that I saw right through his doggone logic and what he said was absolutely right on tar-get, but the intent of his target was not scientific merit. This was clearly an untracker role."*

Note how the interviewee seems to believe that Hal's pri-mary role was that of an untracker. Is it possible that turf war generals bring in the "talent" for critical territorial battles? Just like valuable troubleshooters, there may be gifted untrackers on call to come in when needed to confuse an issue beyond repair. If so, there are many people out there with that aptitude.

Others interviewed came up with similar stories. Most of them still felt emotion about the events they described. They were incredulous that the game had been so logical, so rational, so "right on target" that they had been fooled into bolting off in the wrong direction, damaging their own cause in the process:

"It's the wild goose chase. If they send you off on enough of them, you won't think the thing to be hunted is in their territory. It appears to be so credible. It helps in maintaining territory. If I can get you away from my territory, I win."

Untracking is hidden in the camouflage of support. It can occur at a meeting, or it can be achieved in a series of one-on-one conversations. The untracker need only create a tributary leading away from the goal. The tributary can be an additional preparatory step, an opportunity to bring in a new partner, a bigger application than was previously discussed. Taking this tack, the untracker can get a group to bite off more than it can chew, after which the group will choke on the project or initiative before it can invade protected territory.

Another tack is to stir up an ego battle as a diversionary tactic. In most organizations, it doesn't take much to stir up someone else's turf war. Played effectively, the ego battlers go hell for leather, diverting time and attention away from making progress on the project at hand. Territorial players frequently find emotional "buttons" they can push in order to create the desired wild goose chase. The most effective button of all is the button that activates the perceived invader's own insecurities.

"What Is That Hanging From Your Nose?" and Other Insecurities

Capitalizing on a listener's insecurity is a good way to create confusion. Emotions can hijack the rational mind. Arranging for an opponent's mind to be hijacked clearly creates an advantage for the turf war player. Calling attention to an old embarrassment—an inaccurate sum or a "little brown thing hanging" from her nose—can generate enough emotion to flush her face and her composure at the same time. Making it appear to be credible is all sleight of hand. They were just trying to help. Since no one likes to admit their insecurities, the target is likely to play right into the hands of a camouflage player.

One example demonstrates the tactic of making a discussion so complex and unwieldy that the other side gets lost in the details. The group prefers to simply remain lost rather than ask for clarification and risk looking dumb or out of touch.

> *"Their response was to get more complex. We were lost and they were sounding like experts. They made [the discussion] more complex in order to enhance themselves and sound legitimate."*

If group members had asked counterquestions, these "experts" might have ended up lost in their own complexities. But they didn't because they were afraid they might sound dumb. A truly gifted camouflage player can cause a perceived invader to think "Maybe I don't know what I'm talking about here." When the target is not good with numbers, trotting out tables and charts can do the trick. If he is, metaphors and stretches of the imagination can confuse him. Once the game player instigates discussion around a topic that activates the target's insecurities, he has bought valuable time for other territorial games.

The Diversionary Sneak Attack

Sometimes camouflage can be combined with discrediting. Timing is important. It is a rather complex sequence, but one you are sure to recognize.

In a meeting at which two departments are discussing next year's resource allocations, Department A is just about to make a legitimate point that might threaten the size of next year's budget for Department B. At that moment, B's manager begins to ask questions about the declining profit margins of A's product line. This is a diversionary sneak attack. It comes from nowhere. And the representatives of Department A are completely unprepared to defend themselves.

No one has brought any statistics with them, so there can be no denial of the implications. Thus an accusation not countered by a firm denial hangs in the air. All minds at the meeting are looping back through their memories to retrieve something that might confirm or deny this attack. As they loop, the line item to decrease Department B's budget has been put on hold. All eyes are now turned to the manager of Department A as he scrambles for an explanation. A double play of the camouflage and discredit games decides another battle in an internal turf war.

This double play is a very popular camouflage game. In the following case, the lingering effects proved as powerful as the meeting dynamics. Worried about his own escalating scrap levels, a production manager pointed the finger at the tooling department. In this meeting, he successfully diverted attention away from his own problem and dealt the tooling department a credibility blow in the process:

> *"He had a great deal of pressure put on him at that particular moment in time. His plant manager was more and more upset with the scrap level that he was accumulating. He easily redirected the anger from the plant manager to the engineering manager by suggesting that his performance might have been better had he been getting better service or better tooling from the engineer's organization. The tooling manager was caught off guard. Had he been able to go back and talk to his subordinates and get information to clearly say this wasn't true . . . but all of a sudden he was under fire and he was then the subject of the plant manager's direct anger. It seems to be kind of a game that is played. In the short term, the engineering manager did the best job he could to defend himself. He didn't have the data at hand to be able to do that. He said he would be back, but the meeting was over and everyone left. At the next meeting he attempted to counteract this information again, but at that point in time it was old information. Nobody was particularly interested in listening to it, and they went on with business. The long-term impact was that the situation didn't change. I think that no one really focused on the real problem."*

This is the problem with territorial games. No one really focuses on the real problem. Once the games are set in motion, people focus on the games and the emotions they generate. They can't see the real problem because it is hidden deep within protected territory behind diversionary camouflage. Employee time spent defending against arbitrary accusations wastes time and resources in your organization. Time spent defending against imaginary threats is just as wasteful.

Look Behind You!

Imaginary threats can swivel attention away from the real issue as quickly as an attack does. When a movie villain held at gunpoint gets the hero to believe that there is another villain right behind him, a momentary glance over the shoulder wins the battle. The distraction is enough for the bad guy to grab the gun and the girl and the money, not to mention the balance of power.

While it isn't quite that dramatic on the corporate scene, the objective is the same. A territorial player who can create the perception of a looming threat can distract other employees long enough to kill the new project that would have taken a big chunk out of his perceived territory. In this next situation, information and decision-making privileges were protected turf for a certain group of managers. They liked things the way they were. A new program that would increase accountability was decidedly threatening to their territory. Their territorial game of camouflage focused on imaginary perceptions of danger that would stall and perhaps prevent the implementation of the program.

> *"So it ranged from discounting to actually creating a perception of threats. A new program was positioned to be potentially dangerous to the welfare of the company in order to keep it from affecting the way a group of managers did business."*

Pointing out the dangers, risks, and imaginary boogeymen connected with a new project or initiative can divert attention for long enough. And if it isn't long enough, it can be done again, and again, and again.

Déjà Vu All Over Again

There are many effective methods of creating confusion. Untracking, embarrassing, attacking, scaring—and then there's the time-honored tactic of using them all in a circular motion until the perceived invader gets dizzy. The camouflage player is here, there, and everywhere until everyone is confused.

> *"What he did . . . was anything but what he had publicly said in that first meeting. Because when he came back for the second meeting he's saying they will not support this, that, and the other, and the feeling at the time was that this is what he told them as opposed to what they told him. . . . You had to talk to people to find out who said what. They'd say, 'Dr. So-and-So says this is a critical, key issue on the matter.' But you go do your own research and you find it's different. Then you hear about other actions that didn't fit with the words."*

It can be months after the beginning of a project before people realize that they have been led in circles and are right back where they started. By the time they get their bearings, the turf war may have been won—at their cost.

My, My, How Time Flies

In the next case, the territorial player had only to keep the "opposition" confused long enough to go on vacation.

> *"On the surface he was trying to be—using cognitive kinds of objections—rational. He made a number of what continued to be rational-sounding comments—what he intended to convey were legitimate objections. Then he went on vacation. He has been on vacation ever since. He has been successful so far. I will not press it. It's not worth the hassle from my point of view."*

In today's rapidly changing world, "temporary" solutions that last even six months are permanent enough. It doesn't matter that the tactic won't hold up for very long; none of today's territorial battles *last* very long. A battle can be won or lost in an afternoon—and, in some situations, only an hour.

On the other hand, the war can go on for years. In the following example, strategic noncompliance was combined with camouflage. The manager described, by using excuses and window dressing, was successful in keeping a new salary scheme out of his territory for three years:

> *"After the first year he talked about the fact that it was too late this year and he'd do it next year. And then the next year there were a lot of excuses. He did a little bit to kind of window-dress it a bit. But by the time . . ."*

Often territorial players will create confusion by throwing the responsibility for action back into the lap of the perceived invader. They create the impression of being willing to cooperate . . . if only you would do your part, or arrange to meet these conditions, or find a cure for world hunger, first.

> *"Another way that they avoid coming to some sort of consensus is just to say, well, if you can get my [performance] objective changed, I'll change my behavior. They pass it over to you and say if you can handle the problem . . . then I'll talk to you. . . . It's a wild goose chase, an avoidance tactic. They set it up so it's impossible."*

Smoke and mirrors to confuse an otherwise simple task, process, agreement, whatever action the territorial player perceives as invasive. Camouflage as a territorial game incorporates the art of illusion. Strategies to distract and confuse can come in many forms. Each organization will tend to have a certain style that takes its shape from the values of the group. Sometimes it is an illusion of a better opportunity elsewhere, a threat in need of urgent attention, or an introduction of a new technology that is "almost ready."

If a corporate culture glorifies the trend setters, opportunities are likely to get the dogs running. If it is risk-averse, exaggerating a threat can cloud everyone's thinking at a meeting. When they are all techno-geeks, waiting for the next generation of software or hardware can stall a project for years. The game can be played many, many ways. Each of these is easily defended by arguing the legitimacy of the opportunity, threat, or whatever. While none of the territorial games is easy to pinpoint, the camouflage game is the hardest territorial game to prove and the most difficult to defend against.

THE CAMOUFLAGE GAME SELF-TEST

List the two most important initiatives in process at your organization this year. Under each, list the next step that should be taken to contribute to the progress of this initiative. List the obstacles to this step, specifically itemizing any areas that are so unclear that their lack of clarity prevents progress.

Initiative One: _____ _____ *Next Step:* _____ _____	*Obstacles:* _____ _____ _____ _____
Initiative Two: _____ _____ *Next Step:* _____ _____	*Obstacles:* _____ _____ _____ _____

Initiative One:

Who is helping to replace the confusion with clarity? _____

_____

_____

Who may be contributing to the confusion? _____

_____

_____

What do they (is it you?) stand to gain by letting things stay unclear?

_____

_____

Initiative Two:

Who is helping to replace the confusion with clarity? _____

_____

_____

Who may be contributing to the confusion? _____

_____

_____

What do they (is it you?) stand to gain by letting things stay unclear?

_____

_____

13

The Filibuster Game

We seem to have run out of time.

The game of filibustering is an art unto itself. It is actually a cross between the camouflage game and the occupation game—occupying valuable floor time with confusing rhetoric. Revered on the floors of Congress, the filibuster game is played by talking long enough and sometimes (but not always) eloquently enough to delay any progress that might invade protected territory. Like the other strategies, this one thrives on the appearance of cooperative intent. The social norms of politeness, our formal and informal rules of order in meetings, and our traditional decision-making processes protect the filibuster game player. In our culture, everyone is given the opportunity to have a say. Respect for freedom of speech is so deeply ingrained in some of us that we collaborate with the filibusterer by giving him floor time long after he has taken up more than his fair share. A territorial game player will exploit these deep freedom-of-speech convictions to protect his or her turf.

Eyes may be rolling and side conversations may ridicule this player, but the filibusterer continues to wag his or her tongue until the coast is clear. Once the window of opportunity into the valued territory has passed, hypnotic stares of listeners confirm that they have been effectively immobilized, or someone storms out of the room, further sealing the win for the filibuster game player. Remember, valued territory need only be protected up to the point where "it's just worth it" to the perceived invader.

Some people have a very low tolerance for time wasters. They are easily goaded into an emotional reaction that may loosen their hold on valued territory. The filibusterer often appears shocked and hurt when his opposition huffs out of a meeting and slams the door, but close inspection may reveal a tiny smile of victory. Whether the outcome is delay or an aborted meeting, the filibusterer has still achieved his or her objective. Yet more often, the filibusterer will choose to tap into harmony rather than discord to achieve his or her objectives. The best way to avoid interruptions is to pick a topic with universal appeal.

Motherhood and Apple Pie

Outside of Congress, where rules of order protect speakers from too many interruptions, the favored filibuster topics are usually the issues with which no one disagrees. People are less likely to interrupt a diatribe on the benefits of, say, more money for everyone, more leisure time, or feeding the poor for fear of appearing opposed to such popular ideas. With this built-in protection, a speaker can continue on for much longer.

> *"They were all nodding and agreeing, but I could see we were just wasting our time. No one wanted to be the one to tell him he was full of crap so they just sat and listened to him ramble on. After all, no one could disagree with the fact that we needed to act more like a team. But wasting all this time talking about our values, and customer service, didn't solve the problem. Everyone walked out of that meeting and went right back to the same ole, same ole."*

Frequently, solutions to tough problems mean that someone is going to have to relinquish some turf. It may mean sharing decision-making responsibilities or information or bringing new people into valued relationships. In the example above, the president of the company was hoarding all these "territories." His staff people could not do their jobs without "invading" his territories of decision making, information, and relationships. Protected by his position, he used the filibuster game and many other territorial games to prevent his staff from breaking through the walls he had constructed. Even his one-on-one conversations were marked by the filibuster game. Staff stopped visiting the president's office because not only would he not listen, but they might not get out of there for hours.

The president has since been removed from this position, but the company has not yet recovered from the damage he wrought. His territorial impulses caused the company to lose customers and valuable staff members. It seems that he was totally blind to his territorially driven motivations. As you read this, he is still probably luring people in to listen to his motherhood and apple pie philosophies and then talking their ears off. It is possible that he, himself, was hypnotized by his own rhetoric.

Hypnotizing Rhetoric

In our culture we value verbal skills. Many of those interviewed displayed a grudging admiration for individuals adept at the art of filibuster. The filibuster artist is the one who can make you listen even when you don't agree. He can weave his words like a spider's web to catch a meeting full of flies.

> *"In meetings when they get to the point where the gloves are off, it becomes very, very loud. The loudest and most eloquent—one fellow in particular had an exquisite command of the English language. He could make you listen, even though he was on the other side. He could compel you to listen by his rhetoric. It was beautiful. So well thought out and delivered. You knew he was a snake. You knew full well . . . that what you were hearing was but a tip of the intent, what he was saying was only a portion of what he wanted you to hear. You knew that what came before you on the table did not represent all that there was."*

And yet everyone, including the person who thought he was a "snake," listened. The more compelling the rhetoric is the more powerfully the filibuster game operates as a strategy to defend protected territory. Filibustering can be either conscious or unconscious. Many descriptions of excessive talking created the impression that these territorial players were simply playing for time. However, it is possible that they were totally unaware of the game.

The territorial drive frequently lies beneath conscious awareness. Just as nervousness can cause someone to "run off at the mouth," a territorial anxiety can create the same behavior. The meeting starts to get too close for comfort and before they know it the territorial player has spontaneously climbed onto his or her soapbox and begun to hold forth. Those skilled in rhetoric are more likely to do it often simply because it worked the last time. For instance, the production manager in the example below effectively kept a robotics application out of his factory by using the filibuster game. Without convincing anyone that it genuinely was not an efficient use of resources, he folded up the invasion simply by babbling on and on:

> *"This was about the application of artificial intelligence [robotics] in a plant. The engineering staff people made a presentation. The manufacturing manager and the production manager were very opposed to this particular application. The production manager didn't see the worth of it. He said, 'This isn't going to work and here's why.' He obviously didn't have any data at his fingertips. He didn't have good information to say why it wouldn't work, but he gave a variety of reasons of why we've done things all along this way, and his opinion was that it would waste a lot of money and create more problems than it would solve. He just kept talking. The engineering people kind of folded up their tents and said, 'Well, if you're not willing to listen to new ideas, we're not going to force them down your throat. It's your operation.' And that was the end of that."*

The production manager's reaction was probably automatic. It is unlikely that he walked into that meeting saying to himself, "I think I'll just talk them to death." It was more likely an unconscious response to a vague anxiety. Fear of unforeseen consequences crept up, hijacked his brain, and flipped the on switch to his mouth. Without a territorial drive clouding his judgment, he might have found the new technology to be in his own best interests. Instead, all he saw were invaders, and his tongue seemed to be the best defense at the time.

Not everyone is totally unaware of their behavior when they are playing the filibuster game. Some people purposefully flood the field with words.

Just One More Thing

As with all territorial games, the objective is to protect valued territory. In the filibuster game, protection is achieved by building an impenetrable wall of words. The more logical it sounds to others, the more effective that wall is.

> *"People want to hang on to what they've got. They do it by finding a variety of rationales. Some of it seems very logical as they speak openly in a meeting. On the surface it would seem that it isn't relevant, but you really can't say it isn't until you've really looked at something. There's so many things that are going on at once . . . it really doesn't provide us an opportunity to look at every situation. So they generate so much data that it's impossible to counteract."*

The "logic" is part of the game. It is ironic that logic should be so useful to someone in the grip of an emotional drive. Enough logic can cause listeners to doubt their position and stay quiet while the filibuster player just keeps on going. Anyone who was on the debate team knows that.

The obstacle created through filibuster is a wall of words an invader must break through to get to the protected territory. The dynamic of this strategy lies less in the fact that the words have convinced anyone of their logic as in the fact that the volume of words increases the effort necessary to reevaluate each new approach. Increasing the effort to reach a clear conclusion can block progress for just long enough. Less eloquent filibuster game players use repetition to fill in the time. In the following situation, repetition not only wasted time; it was used to build an argument and wear out an opponent.

> *"Some people might ask a question, and I feel it's already been answered three different ways. The reality is probably*

that they just don't want to do it that way so they just keep asking the question. I always take that as though they are trying to wear the person down that has the issue."

Questions that aren't really questions are used in other territorial games, like the discredit or camouflage game. In the filibuster game, questions can be used to create repetitive loops or to activate the "talker" of the group.

Let's Hear From Mr. Gushmouth

Sophisticated filibuster players can save their vocal cords by inducing others to unwittingly participate in this delay tactic. Asking the guy who never shuts up what he thinks about the issue, mentioning the CEO's favorite monologue topic, or stimulating an old disagreement between two other group members can set off a stream of verbiage guaranteed to have nothing to do with the matter at hand. Every group has a Mr. or Ms. Gushmouth who loves to hear the sound of his or her own voice.

"I could've killed her when she turned to him and asked what he thought. This was none of his business. He didn't have a clue what we should do, but that didn't bother him. His ego was so pumped up that he didn't realize she was just using him."

Territory can change so rapidly that timing is critical in a corporate turf war. Ten minutes of rambling can win a battle. The filibuster game rarely wins the entire territorial war, but it can be used strategically to weaken the perceived invader's chances.

In a serious turf war, many battles are decided in a meeting. The decision to go ahead on a project, to stop a project, to fund or not fund development may all represent emotionally charged territorial wins or losses to someone. Once a meeting slips into an adversarial situation, filibustering can buy valuable time for a territorial player.

THE FILIBUSTER GAME SELF-TEST

In your next regular staff meeting or project meeting, ask the permission of everyone involved to do this experiment. *Once they agree,* list the names of all who attend (yours included) and circulate a copy, asking that everyone be rated in order from "Talks too much" to "Talks too little." Explain that the information is part of an exercise to increase collaboration in the meeting. You must ensure anonymity in order to get honest results. Sealed, unmarked envelopes sent to a truly neutral (and trustworthy) administrative person will usually satisfy most people. Ask this person to tabulate the answers and provide a list of the top two and bottom two talkers from the lists.

If your name *is not* on the "Talks too much" list: Present the findings as a group exercise. Ensure that the talkers don't feel attacked (or they could slide into malicious obedience). Help the ones who don't talk enough to understand how much people want and need their contribution. Use the results to encourage discussion about improving group collaboration. Explain the filibuster game and ask if this could be part of the motivation to "talk too much." Don't forget that even those who rarely speak up can play the filibuster game. A territorial threat can activate even the shyest introvert. Ask group members if they can remember other instances of the filibuster game.

If your name *is* on the "Talks too much" list: It is time to do a little self-examination. Could you be guilty of using the filibuster game in these meetings in order to get your way, keep others out, or protect your turf? If so (and it is likely if your name is at the top of the list), present the findings as described above and demonstrate to the group your willingness to stop playing the filibuster game by not making excuses and by hereafter making a genuine effort to keep quiet.

Warning: NEVER, NEVER gather information like this without circulating it as soon as possible. If you think that you might not want to share the results, don't ask for the information in the first place. Gathering information of this sort and refusing to share it builds internal barriers that can cause significant damage.

14

Serious Sabotage

The sniper.

Most of the games described here either indirectly deliver a blow to a perceived invader, create a covert obstacle, or muddy the waters in order to confuse the issue. In most situations, even when they do significant damage, they are not intended to "destroy." Emotions may be running high, but they aren't extreme. The games are intended more to inconvenience than to kill. The psychological territory that drives territorial game players is important but usually not so compelling that they go off the deep end.

However, there are times when a turf war escalates to the point where the game players *do* go off the deep end. The movie *Disclosure*, if viewed through the lens of territorial games, is a good example of taking the turf war a bit too far. A message saying that a meeting had been moved back instead of forward put a character in the job-threatening position of being an hour late for a critical meeting. This was a double play uniting the discredit and information manipulation games. But at this level, this was no game. This was serious sabotage.

Most territorial games come from unconscious impulses. The purpose of my research and this book has been to highlight the petty little games that are played unknowingly—games that are played without any conscious consideration for the consequences. Yet it would be irresponsible to leave the discussion of territorial games without addressing the dangerous minority of

individuals who use these tactics ruthlessly and with full awareness.

Not Just a Game

Most territorial battles are fought well within the societal norms
and parameters of fairness and civility. The territorial players
who do not play within these boundaries are sabotage players.
The actions of saboteurs dance on the fringes of these social parameters. They make guerrilla strikes and then hide in the safety
of the behavioral gray areas.

Sabotage is strikingly proactive. Other strategies may or
may not come from a conscious territorial urge, but sabotage is
always conscious, malicious, and stealthy. As I did the research,
I found that sabotage could have been grouped into any of the
other game categories. Yet some of the stories told to me were
too strong to be labeled the intimidation *game,* the information
manipulation *game,* or the strategic noncompliance *game.*

Technically, the pattern of behavior was the same: Intimidation, misleading information, or an unkept agreement excluded
a perceived invader in some way from the protected territory or
frightened her away. But in these stories, the perceived invader's
retreat was marked by a pronounced limp or other evidence of
permanent damage. The intensity of the games demands that
they be treated separately.

Sabotage is playing territorial hardball. People who are not
wanted in a territory are given impossible jobs—the equivalent
of corporate Siberia. Resources are withheld in a manner that
not only inconveniences them but literally prevents them from
doing their jobs. Certain cost centers get saddled with expenses
that make them liable for legal action. Gossip is so destructive
that not only is a promotion out of the question but a person is
fired.

The intensity of the sabotage is evident in the language used
to describe it:

> *"They were trying to get rid of the weak ones. They starved
> them out."*

"He ran into a lot of traps. He didn't have a chance."

"This person really didn't want confrontation—it was all underground. She was going to do what she could to destroy me."

On the positive side, there were not as many anecdotes that fit this category. The ones that did exuded a lasting bitterness that proves how important our territory can be. Access to prestigious jobs, the high esteem of our peers, lucrative business opportunities can give a life-or-death intensity to territorial battles.

Big Stakes

Sabotage may mean winning turf that has no value for the territorial player. Sometimes the games escalate to the point where there is no obvious territorial benefit for the "turf lord." The emotions created by a territorial urge are extreme and have taken over a player's rational faculties to a degree that can only be likened to a territorial feeding frenzy. Emotions like fear, anger, and desire spiral out of control. When this happens the game may turn into sabotage.

In one situation, a professor felt an administrator's sting of sabotage after the professor did not agree to apply grant money to the administrator's pet project. The successful professor had a contract sanctioning his thriving consulting business outside of his academic responsibilities. He was guaranteed free days so that he could augment his professor's salary. This money was important to him, and in a sabotage play the administrator played the invisible wall game to the point where an important source of the professor's livelihood was cut off:

"I was entitled to a day a week consulting. I was doing stuff and he really hated it. He just did not like the fact that I had a consulting business. He was jealous. He did something that in all the years I was there he never had done to me. He scheduled my spring semester without asking me. He gave me a class on every day of the week. So then I had no free days. He absolutely did it on purpose. He was real nasty."

Nastiness is delivered with piercing accuracy. Sabotage is the territorial felony; the other strategies are misdemeanors in comparison. Because of its impact, sabotage is harder to disguise. It is more difficult to explain away as unintentional. And often enough, it backfires. The manager quoted below fired the sabotaging surbordinate described here:

> *"I was on the road a lot and things would happen and I would not be given information. I would go into meetings and look like a fool because this person would not give me feedback. . . . Of course our EVP at the time was totally furious with me because I should have known what was going on. . . . This was not incompetence. She had such a desire to feel powerful . . . so she played 'I know something you don't know.' "*

To those caught unaware, the sabotage play can come as quite a surprise.

From Left Field

The element of surprise often enhances the effectiveness of a serious sabotage play and simultaneously protects the saboteur (at least temporarily) from retaliation. The sniper who strikes without warning in a meeting, firing a lethal shot at a program, has most assuredly considered the timing of the shot. The manager described below didn't want an outside consultant coming in to do a study, but nevertheless he allowed the study to go ahead. While superficially agreeing to cooperate, he patiently waited for his opportunity to sabotage it. Finally, when the results were presented, the manager attacked every conclusion and effectively prevented the presentation from continuing.

> *"So the study was commissioned and done. When it was done, the consultant came in to present it and was brutalized by the top management guy. He castrated the guy."*

Needless to say, the recommendations were never enforced and the money spent on the study might as well have gone for corporate manicures for all the impact it had on productivity.

Since sabotage is a question of degree, identifying it depends on the situation and the culture of the organization in which it occurs. The important point to remember is that sabotage is a good indication that territorial urges have gotten out of hand and have probably eclipsed rational attention to the organization's goals and objectives. Serious sabotage means that the turf war is no longer a game and that someone is going to get hurt.

When a turf war has escalated to the point of serious sabotage, there is precious little to do but choose sides and hope your side wins. Solutions will require the corporate version of the United Nations, peace agreements, and probably peacekeeping forces.

Fortunately, most turf wars are not so serious. They are a drain on productivity, they pervert the organization's goals, but no one dies. As long as the turf war has not escalated to this point, there are practical solutions to territorial games. The chapters in Part Three give you clear descriptions of several workable options that can be used to counteract turf wars and territorial games in your organization.

There is one catch, however. First, we start on you and *your* territorial drives and behaviors. Sure, those bozos at the office may have started it, but you haven't got a prayer of deescalating a turf war until you become aware of your contributions to the battle. Be honest with yourself as you do the next exercise and see if any of your own games have escalated to the level of sabotage.

Serious Sabotage Self-Test

Write a paragraph that describes the one person you consider to be most dangerous to your career plans and aspirations. Describe in detail the actions this person could possibly take to sabotage your success. Don't worry about sounding paranoid; just write.

_____

_____

_____

_____

_____

_____

Now identify the areas where you could do him some damage. What actions could you take to sabotage his success? What countermeasures have you considered *just in case* he did something to you?

_____

_____

_____

Be honest with yourself. Have you initiated any of these actions? Have you alluded to the possibility of taking action? Have you given anyone else a nudge to take one of these actions?

_____

_____

_____

If so, you may be unaware that you are playing a sabotage-level game.

What damage could occur if this game continued? What is the potential loss to the organization?

_____

_____

_____

What might happen if you called a truce? How would your organization benefit?

_____

_____

_____

Part Three
Ending Turf Wars

15

Tearing Down the Walls

"If you want to succeed you should strike out on new paths, rather than travel the worn paths of accepted success."

—John D. Rockefeller, Sr.

How many books have you read about management, leadership, and organizational culture? And how many have made a significant difference to your behavior or to the behavior of those around you? Did you just read these books and pound the table with your fist, or did you go out and do something different? This section of the book is about doing something different. There are many things you can do to decrease the frequency and intensity of territorial games.

Doing Something

Eliminating them is impossible (and not very smart). As long as we have limited resources, there will always be some level of territoriality. And you need to take care of yourself out there; part of the territorial drive is an overwhelming desire to keep your job. However, the game-y side of territoriality in which emotion overrides reason is *not* taking care of yourself. It is a mindless exclusion of people who are really on your side or could easily be on your side.

Territorial boundaries, infighting, and internal turf wars

don't help your organization or the individuals in your organization. In the bigger picture, they are no longer survival-smart behaviors. Rapid-paced change, information overload, and the global economy have changed our environment, and we humans need to adapt. As we become more interdependent we need new behaviors that facilitate our interdependence. Hoarding information, excluding workmates, and covert sabotage only destroy our chances for success in this new environment.

Eventually, natural selection will take care of things. Overly territorial organizations will die out. But, personally, I would recommend being a little more proactive. You can consciously choose to evolve beyond these primitive territorial games. It isn't easy; decreasing territorial games can be scary, emotional, and difficult. But the payoff makes the struggle worth it. There is nothing more fun than working with a team that has torn down the barriers. Team members are creative, excited, and thrilled with their own abilities. Information flows and work does too. Unfortunately, territorial games rarely disappear spontaneously.

It will take effort to deescalate territorial games in your organization. Your job, as you read the next few chapters, is to decide specifically what you will do to help bring about change—not what those other jerks should be doing. What are *you* going to do this week and next week to make a difference?

It is possible that there is nothing you can do. Some organizations are so full of fear, anger, and greed that you might as well skip this part and use Chapters 4 through 14 as a playbook. In that sort of environment, playing territorial games may be necessary until significant cultural shifts occur. However, the territorial games in your organization are probably closer to bad habits than compulsive patterns. Bad habits are curable.

The first draft of this section lies in a garbage dump somewhere. In that draft, I wanted to be very, very clear. However, I found that as my recommendations became clearer they moved further away from what I know works. Since human behavior is confusing, any discussion of human behavior mirrors that confusion. I had to choose between workable recommendations that allow for some of that confusion and nice, tight, clear recommendations that probably wouldn't work. I chose to give you the stuff I know works, with complete confidence that you are smart enough to adapt it to your unique situation and work out your own clarity.

There are no recipes for changing a territorial culture. Because every situation is different, each solution will be different. You are the best one to decide when, where, and how to use what is presented in this book. Be creative. Chop and change. Bend and adapt.

But do something.

Designing Your Own Solutions

Following are guidelines from which you can design your own solution. More than likely, you don't have as much power over the structure of your organization as you would like to have, but that doesn't make you powerless. These strategies are designed to be implemented at any level, with two people or with a group. Start where you are and design your own solutions for increasing cooperation and bringing down internal boundaries.

What *Doesn't* Work: Mandating Cooperation

OK, we know that territoriality exists. We have a name for it. We agree that it is counterproductive. So on the count of three, everyone STOP DOING IT!

You have just experienced one of the fundamental unpleasant truths about changing behavior. Recognizing a behavior, knowing that it is not in your best interests, and then rationally deciding to change it doesn't work very well. We humans are more complex than that. If it were that simple, no one would smoke, drink too much, or have unprotected sex. We would all weigh five pounds less than the charts say we should weigh, and I would be reading three periodicals a day and have my Christmas cards out by the first of December.

Let it go, people. It is pure fantasy to believe that a vision statement and a list of values distributed throughout the organization and pasted on the walls can successfully mandate collaboration across territorial lines. Try it one more time if you want to, but you will probably find that the new program of the month works only as well as the last program of the month did.

Cooperation stems from a complex assortment of reasons. Each individual cooperates for a variety of different reasons. Most of these reasons are emotionally based and incorporate some degree of self-interest or self-image.

When faced with emotional behavior, too many people are quick to throw up their hands and declare any attempt to change these behaviors a waste of time. It is true that territorial games are deeply ingrained and rooted in emotion. You are tackling powerful dynamics when you seek to decrease territorial games.

At the core of these territorial games is an emotion-generating instinct. Territoriality is an instinct designed for survival. It is only natural for humans to seek out similar others and to cling to whatever valuable assets they can secure in order to survive and thrive. Counteracting our impulses to keep "what is ours" safe from others means tackling thousands of years of evolutionary and/or cultural programming. Your solution may mean that you are asking human beings to behave in a way that is contrary to their nature, to rise above a basic instinct. It may be difficult, but it is not impossible.

Your organization is composed of an entirely unique collection of individuals with varying degrees of territorial impulses (including yours). The last few years have produced certain territorial patterns of behavior. Each of you has a mental map of territorial lines, your favorite games to protect those lines, and your own defensive reasoning that lets you stay self-righteous about your behavior. A solution means that you are asking yourself and others to drop these defenses, erase security-based lines of territory, and give up familiar habits. Some would be tempted to declare the task impossible—a waste of time.

But it *is* possible and it *is* worth the effort.

It is not a waste of time if you can increase the amount of cooperation you get from your co-workers. If you can be sure that you will receive more of the information you need, when you need it, if you can feel certain that agreements will be kept, if you can create relationships that are supportive regardless of departmental lines, it is not a waste of time.

Your biggest challenge will be to get people to see their behavior for what it is. Right now they feel entirely justified in playing their games and some even feel that their very survival depends on it. Change will depend on how well you can disrupt the old habits and patterns that are now in place. Presumably, you have already experienced the futility of imposed policies. Sending out a memo describing the ten territorial games along with a decree that they will no longer be tolerated is likely to inspire either a finger-pointing session or an e-mail to Scott Adams offering material for a new *Dilbert* cartoon. If you want people to stop playing these territorial games, you'll need to lay some groundwork so they actually want to change their behavior.

Making Them *Want* to Change Their Behavior

How many therapists does it take to change a lightbulb? Only one, but the lightbulb has to *want* to change. At least lightbulbs have a fairly predictable range of options—they are either on or off. People have a thousand on/off switches tied to a thousand unconscious patterns of behavior. Ask two people the same question and one will jump to answer it while the other jumps to the defense. Not because of the question *you* asked, but because of *their* habits (or how they have programmed themselves). If they are programmed to be territorial and jump to the defense, your attempts to force them to change their behavior will only accelerate their territorial games.

Any attempt to *make* someone change will inevitably be seen as a serious encroachment into their psychological territory. If they are territorial in the first place, any forced solution will just make things worse. You will only create more games—like the discredit game or the strategic noncompliance game. You may even think you are making progress . . . in the beginning. Territorial games are too covert to see all at once. But eventually, forcing people just results in more territorial games.

The solutions you design must not be intrusive. Rather than setting out to make anyone change, set out to make that person *want* to change. If you want someone to change an emotionally generated pattern, you need access to the trigger/response programming inside his or her own mind. Trust me, the easiest way is for *them* to identify and isolate the trigger and their response pattern. People are too complex to understand without their cooperation and they are too difficult to change without their permission. Since people only change their behavior for one reason, because they *want* to change it, it is your responsibility to create a genuine desire for change.

For example, there is nothing worse than running a team-building session for a bunch of people who don't want to be there. In our consulting practice we always lay the groundwork for any process before we begin. Experience with groups like the business intelligence group for a reengineered utility company has taught us this lesson. This utility company had reengineered two departments into one, which would share a pool of adminis-trative support staff. They had been commanded to attend a Sat-urday session on team building, and none of them wanted to be there. They demonstrated their resentment with arguments and sarcasm, and one person even leaned back in her chair and audi-bly counted the ceiling tiles while we discussed the agenda. Continuing in this atmosphere would have done more damage than good. We threw away the agenda and the group spent the next two hours looking for an outcome that might justify the sacrifice of a Saturday.

Eventually group members decided that clearing the air be-tween themselves and their new boss would be worth it. With this new goal, the whole room changed. They *wanted* to be there. We accomplished the same outcome of team building, but it was much, much easier after the group designed its own reasons for doing it. We laid the groundwork first, and then introduced new options for behavior. Two years later, they still credit that session with building a successful team environment.

Of course, it helps to be a trained facilitator. Laying the groundwork is easier with a background in psychology, coun-seling, and behavioral science. But it isn't impossible for the lay-person. Even if you aren't a trained facilitator, there are tactics and strategies you can use to reduce the amount of territorial games being played in your work group or your entire organiza-tion.

Understanding the Behaviors You Want to Change

Organizations change one individual at a time. Sure, it is easier to draw flowcharts and new organizational structures than to consider individuals and their unique patterns of behavior. And many management issues can be improved with these big-picture, logic-based methods, but territorial games fall into the arena of emotional behavior. Using tools that were designed for rational and logic-based systems on the irrational and emotion-based system of human behavior will only lead to inaccurate conclusions and solutions that may do more harm than good.

Many managers, in good faith, sit in their offices designing and redesigning their departments until they find the "perfect solution." A well-meaning manager can sit in his office and draw and redraw boxes and arrows until he is sure his new allocation of responsibilities, division of tasks, and redirection of work flow will increase the productivity of the entire department. He can then enthusiastically introduce his perfect solution to his staff, implement the changes, and two months later wonder what in the hell happened. Nine times out of ten, it just doesn't go as he planned.

What happens? Instead of embracing the perfect solution, Susie gets so irritated that Frank, the new guy, was introduced into "her" project that she accidentally-on-purpose lets the ball drop just to make Frank look bad. Chris's ego gets out of hand as the new project manager. He micromanages to the point that John and Terry spend more time putting him "in his place" than they spend working. And the three positions that were eliminated just turn up somewhere else. It was such a perfect solution! It was perfect on paper. It was perfectly logical. It was perfectly rational. And it was a disaster when imposed upon perfectly illogical, irrational, emotional human beings. Seen through the lens of human territorial drives, many perfect solutions just don't make sense.

Working With What You Have

In the realm of human behavior, our financial and business analysis training will hamper our ability to see what is really there. We become blind to whatever doesn't make sense for the simple reason that it doesn't make sense. Unfortunately, the behaviors that don't make sense are sabotaging your opportunity to increase cooperative effort and cross-functional team productivity.

If something can't be analyzed with our existing tools, we disregard it. That's too bad because few businesspeople possess the analytical tools designed for application to the realm of human behavior.

So, forget your precious logic when you approach territorial behaviors. See the behaviors through the lens of psychologic. Consider how fear and anger can stay beneath a person's conscious thoughts and activate old patterns like the territorial games described here. Know that emotional behavior is not the enemy. It is *unexamined* emotional behavior that wreaks havoc. Use what you understand about emotion and survival instincts to design your intervention.

Never try to change a behavior at the level of the behavior. You must go beneath the surface to find the motivating force behind that behavior. Addressing a behavior without altering the motivating force is like moving a ball attached to a rubber band. It will stay there as long as you hold it, but let it go and the rubber band pulls it right back to where it was before. Ensure that your solution goes deep into the belief system running emotions and you will find the leverage you need for lasting change.

Also, be very judicious in using the word *should* when you think or talk about territorial behavior. In my experience, whenever people talk about how things *should* be, or how others *should* feel or act, then they aren't working with reality. Telling your team members that they *should* work more cooperatively is a waste of breath. Think about it this way. You are heading off to California and you have two maps: One map shows where all the U.S. highways *should* be and the other map shows where they really are. Which map are you going to use? Telling people how they should behave is like using the map where the roads should be. You end up lost and irritable and with no one to blame but yourself. Work with what you have instead of what you wish you had. Once you do that, you will be ready to lay some groundwork for behavioral change.

Mapping the Terrain

Before you begin you need to pick your target. Where are the divisive boundaries in your organization? In the empty frame in

Figure 2, create a map of the territorial lines in your organization like the one in Chapter 2. As you draw your map, use any metaphors that occur to you—terrain, architecture, stereotypes, and so on. If you don't consider yourself a visual person, use Africa or Europe as a framework. Consider which parts of your organization might be the Hutus or the Tutsis. If you are using Europe, what division is France, Italy, the Czech Republic, Bosnia, Serbia, or the former Soviet Union? Who represents the United Nations peacekeeping force? If you are living in a *Star Trek* environment, who are the Klingons? Be creative.

This exercise is designed to overcome any natural desire on your part to pretend that these lines are not there—at least not around *your* area (and by the way, possessive pronouns are a dead giveaway that the lines *are* there). Let yourself ham it up. Draw a caricature that exaggerates the divisions and the characteristics of each territory. There is no harm in exaggerating the lines on the map you draw as long as you remember you are using a magnifying glass. The greater risk is to deny that territorial lines exist.

Figure 2. Your Metaphor Map of the Corporate Terrain

No one individual can accurately map the territorial lines because each map reflects the unique viewpoint of the territory from which it is formed. The most useful map will fold together many perspectives. As you progress through this process, you will want to ask other people in your group to draw a map too. I highly recommend the group exercise of creating a collaborative map from individual maps. (Just be sure that all group members draw their individual maps first. Otherwise your group map will reflect either the most dominant group member or the best artist.)

Designing Your Intervention

Once you have identified the battle zones, you can begin to design your intervention. I assume that you are either a change agent or a member of a group using this book as a behavior change tool. I recommend coming together in one room as a cross-sectional group from competing territories. I find that people are usually very interested in talking about territorial issues, so it shouldn't be too hard. Any group should ultimately design and implement its own solutions. The process will in all probability take several meetings over a period of up to six months.

If you are addressing a new merger situation, I strongly recommend letting the dust settle for at least six months before talking about territorial games. Addressing the problem too early can fuel feelings of division and accentuate the differences. Also, in a new merger situation, no one has yet experienced enough inconvenience or irritation to warrant an interest in decreasing territorial games. In a merger situation, it is better to use the territory-building exercises presented in Chapter 18 first, and save the discussions of territorial games for later. However, for all other situations, the process begins with several "breaking down" steps before the "building up" steps can be tackled.

If you are an organizational change agent, you can either prepare your own material or use this book as a group study tool. Whether you choose to facilitate the group, are in a group that has chosen a self-directed approach, or are working on one particular relationship, the processes and exercises in the next chapters will provide a menu of paths from which to choose.

From now on, I will address you as the change agent because, even if you do not formally hold that position, I believe you can make a difference if you want to.

Just don't try to do it alone. Territorial behavior *must* be addressed by a group. If that group consists of only you and the one person you wish would stop playing games, that's fine. But remember, territoriality is a group behavior. No one is territorial in a vacuum. For lasting change, the whole group must change at the same time. If one person changes and the rest of the group doesn't, at best it will have no effect and at worst the changed individual could get eaten alive. The whole group needs to decide to change together.

You, as an individual, can't change a group's behavior. You can set it up for the group to change its own behavior, but you can't change it for them. This may seem obvious, but I've seen people go out there and try anyway. They get impatient. They try to force it.

In the case of territorial games, patience is particularly important because only an impartial observer or the game player herself (which is less likely) can successfully identify a territorial game for what it is. Anyone on the receiving end of these games will only brand himself a whiner or a wimp if he tries to point out the destructive nature of the games. Think about it. If you go out there crying, "Those guys are shunning me," you come off sounding like a wimp.

In a group, there will be enough people so that all members of the group can act as impartial observers of each other. In a group, you can use the group dynamics to override labels like *whiner* and *wimp*. In an "I'll argue your case if you argue mine" arrangement, no one sounds like a whiner and the issues still get addressed. Since this rarely happens spontaneously, you must lay enough groundwork for the group to choose to do this.

Laying the Groundwork

In my own consulting practice, I have found that strategies and tactics that help to loosen old habits and reduce defenses are of more value than the most perfect solution. These are what I call the "breaking down" steps. When people are so set in their ways that they are unwilling to use a perfect solution, then it isn't a perfect solution—it's a useless solution. Consider some of the failed total quality implementations. There is little argument that Deming's seven tools are good tools for group analysis. The fishbone diagram and Pareto chart alone have helped many teams see solutions that otherwise they would have missed. Yet many companies that provided training in these tools found that the training did not transfer to on-site use of the tools. Why? Trainers presented the knowledge, but they did not prepare the group to receive it. I have interviewed company people from professional staff to factory workers who knew very well how to use these tools and didn't, because they didn't want to use them. Again, change only happens when enough people want it to happen. Too many organizational change agents neglect this difficult aspect of implementing a new system of behavior. Old behaviors have to be broken down before new ones can be introduced. Before introducing a solution, people need to believe that there *is* a problem. They need to believe that it is *their* problem. They need to *want* change in order to want *to change.*

Finding Behavioral Options
Within the Comfort Zone

We all have a comfort zone of behavioral options that powerfully direct our choice of behaviors tomorrow toward being what they were today and yesterday. Territorial games are comfort-giving. To the individual playing them, they mean protection, survival, success. Any solution you propose to people in the habit of playing territorial games has to compete with the perceived comfort offered by these games. In order to change, they need to conclude that yesterday's behaviors no longer promise comfort for tomorrow. Only then can you offer new behaviors, and these must promise even higher levels of protection, survival, and success.

Other books have been written on the powerful allure of the comfort zone. Old habits die hard. Because our minds are designed to repeat patterns, our minds repeat patterns. Not good patterns necessarily, just familiar patterns. Event, emotion, behavior; event, emotion, behavior; event, emotion, behavior; and so on indefinitely. There is no reason involved, just familiar patterns. Anyone who has tried to quit smoking or to lose weight can testify to the power of habit over reason. Sheer familiarity has a powerful influence over behavior.

Talking sense to people who are deeply involved in a turf war and playing territorial games is usually a waste of time. They are deeply involved in an event, emotion, behavior pattern that has become a habit. Reason is not an effective way to combat habit, particularly territorial habits, which are not only familiar but emotionally tied to security. When emotions are in play, the application of reason is of limited value. No solution can ignore the power that instinctual impulses and habits hold over our behavior. Your solution must first disrupt old habits and old emotional wiring before introducing anything new.

Implementing a solution to territorial games without doing the groundwork is like painting a masterpiece on a canvas that has not been properly prepared. It looks great at first. But the paint begins to crack and peel and you end up with a bigger mess than when you started. Properly preparing people for change may be agony to the impatient, but it is an absolute necessity for sustained change. If you don't lay the groundwork you could do more harm than good. People have had enough of empty promises and abandoned initiatives.

16

Ripping Up the Foundations

"Let him that would move the world move first himself."
—Socrates

Changing behavior requires going beneath the surface and stirring things up a bit. The map you drew is anchored in deeply rooted foundations called beliefs. Here's a warning: Since territorial games are generated by emotions, be prepared to run into some emotion as you instigate change. Remember, you are asking people to lower their defenses and erase lines that represent security and protection to them. You will probably run into all three of the territorial emotions: fear, anger, and desire. Each of these emotions is an entirely appropriate response to a change in territorial habits. There is no way to bring down internal barriers without some people feeling scared, others getting angry, and a select few rubbing their hands together to grab what they can. If you aren't seeing some emotion, either your solution isn't working or there wasn't a problem in the first place.

Somewhere along the line something happened to cause these people to conclude that playing territorial games was the best way to survive. You probably won't have to look too far for that something. That experience supports the three core beliefs that hold territorial patterns in place. As long as these beliefs hold firm, people will continue to protect their turf. Interventions that target only the visible evidence of the games without targeting these core beliefs will simply drive the games deeper beneath the surface. Lasting behavior change requires changing core beliefs. This requires more than a training session or a bit of discussion time.

Disrupting Old Beliefs and Old Habits

Beliefs come from experience. Disrupting a belief means creating an experience that disproves the old belief and then cementing this *disconfirming* experience by laying down a new belief before the opportunity has passed. In my consulting practice, I use a shortcut for this step—a simulation exercise designed to highlight the short-term, counterproductive, negative effects of territorial behaviors by providing immediate feedback and the direct experience of these negative effects. In other words, I let them embarrass themselves by getting them to recognize that they play a simulation the same way they play business. Overheads and workbooks roll right off the emotional memory, but experience sticks. Experience is the fastest way to change someone's beliefs. You don't have to use a simulation to create experiences. Every interaction you have with others is an experience. Use yourself as a tool to create experiences that change beliefs.

Which beliefs need changing? There are three basic beliefs that hold territorial games in place. These beliefs support the walls that separate us into divisive territories. Each of these three beliefs must be disrupted before territorial games will diminish. They are:

Belief 1: Everyone plays territorial games, so I have to too.
Belief 2: We pretend we aren't playing territorial games.
Belief 3: *They* are the problem, not me.

The people whom you wish were less territorial/more cooperative may not even be aware of these beliefs. Psychological research has long documented that most people don't think about *why* they do the things they do (until long after, and then they are usually making up excuses). Many people profess to believe one thing and then say and do another. So don't expect people to have a conscious awareness of these beliefs or their behaviors. Just keep in mind that if they are playing territorial games, they have some version of these three beliefs hidden in their mental programming.

If you want them to change, you'll have to come up with some sort of experience that will loosen these beliefs enough so that they are willing to try something new. Logical discussion is of limited use with the emotional brain. The emotional brain requires proof (experience). Retraining the emotional brain means providing experiences that *prove* that cooperating is better than playing territorial games. If you want to shake the belief loose, then you must provide some sort of experience that proves the belief false.

Belief 1: Everyone plays territorial games, so I have to too.

Counterproof: I don't play them and I'm not exploited.

The most important first step in any intervention is to walk your talk. If you can't change your own behavior, you can forget about changing theirs. You and your behavior can be the experience that disconfirms their belief that they *have* to play territorial games.

You First

There are few more powerful methods of training than a simple demonstration. A discussion about operating a piece of machinery is never as good as walking someone over to the machine and showing him how to run it. It is the same with behavioral skills. If you want to teach a new skill, show them. Find a way to demonstrate *not* being territorial. It may mean orchestrating a contrived demonstration, but that's OK. If there is no shame in demonstrating a piece of equipment, why should it be any different to demonstrate a behavioral skill? If you feel that it wouldn't be genuine, then you've missed the point about walking your talk. It had *better* be genuine—and meaningful. You may want to share some information earlier than people would expect, include others in an important decision, or invite a peer along the next time you spend time building one of your most important relationships.

A construction executive, who frequently found himself competing for bids that fell into a gray area between his and another business unit's designated area, invited the president of the "competing" business unit to meet with a new prospect whose project clearly fell into that fiercely contested gray area. Once he got over the shock of being included, the two of them ended up discussing a partnering arrangement that capitalized on the strengths of both subunits. This one action avoided months of duplicated effort and covert sabotage that had traditionally characterized their competition for bids in this gray area. By sharing his relationship with the prospect early on, the executive disrupted the territorial patterns they had followed for years. Acting as if they were on the same team won them the confidence of the prospect, and saved a lot of wasted internal competition besides. If you want to change someone else's territorial behaviors, you must be willing to lead the way. If you demonstrate how to fake cooperation, all they will learn is how to fake it—and not to trust you.

Overcoming your territorial impulses is a behavioral skill. That construction executive had to override his first impulse to meet secretly with the prospect and try to win the whole job for himself. Having the skill means feeling an emotional response, feeling the impulse to play a territorial game, and yet deciding not to play it. It is the ability to share information with a co-worker when a nagging anxiety (fear) tells you to withhold it. It means biting your tongue when a sarcastic comment bubbles up in a meeting or speaking up with a clear "no" when you'd just as soon let them discover your noncompliance later on. It is fundamentally a skill of self-management. It is a skill of being inclusive rather than exclusive, open rather than defensive, and cooperative rather than conspiratorial.

It is possible that you have already mastered this skill. It is even possible that you have gone overboard and are in danger of being exploited because you are too cooperative. However, my experience tells me that the vast majority of people need to decrease their own territorial games first before marching off on a mission to change others. Use your own judgment. But I would encourage you to begin your quest to decrease territorial games first with yourself and then move out from there. If you *can* find a behavior to change, it will dramatically increase your credibility with co-workers and thus your ability to influence their behavior.

What Games Do You Play?

Scan your own motivations and find your territorial drive. You've got one. If you don't understand your own territorial drive, you can't accurately see the drives in others. Look at the map you drew of your organization. Consider the boundaries that you protect and the ones that you observe. What games get played between you and those outside your territory? Use the self-tests from Chapters 4 through 14 to help you complete the chart in Figure 3. This survey can be used with your group as well. Make a check mark for every instance over the last three months in which you have experienced one of the ten territorial games described, whether it was used on you, used by a peer, used by your boss, or played by you.

Find someone you can trust to be objective and ask him which territorial games he thinks you play. Even this conversation will require some groundwork. Telling you the truth is risky. The person you select will likely try to point to justifications for your behavior or to all those jerks who are much worse than you. Explain to him that for right now you are more concerned with understanding your *own* territorial behaviors and ask him to help you find the situations in which *you* play territorial games. Once you have identified the areas in which you play territorial games, you can choose when and how you will stop playing those games.

This will provide a forum for you to demonstrate the skill of transcending territorial impulses. Coincidentally, you will find that you play your games with the people who irritate you the most with their games. Choosing cooperation over territorial games with these individuals is the first step to disconfirming their belief that everyone plays these games. It might be risky, but weigh the benefits to you both if you can stop the games.

A word of warning: Don't be naïve and allow yourself to be exploited. Choose circumstances in which there is hope of a cooperative response and always have a contingency plan. When

Figure 3. Understanding Your Own Territorial Drive

Territorial Games	*Used on You*	*Used by Your Peers*	*Used by Your Boss*	*Used by You*
1. Occupation Marking territory; maintaining an imposing physical presence; acting as the gatekeeper for vital information; monopolizing relationships, resources, or information				
2. Information Manipulation Withholding information, putting a "spin" on information, covering up, or giving false information				
3. Intimidation "Growling," yelling, staring someone down, scaring off, or making threats (veiled or overt)				
4. Powerful Alliances Using relationships with powerful people to intimidate, impress, or threaten others; using name dropping; making strategic displays of influence over important decision makers				
5. Invisible Wall Actively instigating circumstances or creating counterproductive perceptions so that an agreed-upon concept is, if not impossible to implement, very, very difficult to implement				
6. Strategic Noncompliance Agreeing up front to take action and having no intention of taking that action, or agreeing just to buy time to find a way to avoid taking that action				
7. Discredit Using personal attacks or unrelated criticisms as a way of creating doubt about another person's competence or credibility				
8. Shunning Subtly (or not so subtly) excluding an individual in a way that punishes him; orchestrating a group's behavior so that another is treated like an outsider				
9. Camouflage Creating a distraction, emphasizing the inconsequential, or deliberately triggering someone's anxiety buttons just to distract him or her				
10. Filibuster Using excessive verbiage to prevent action, outtalking any objectors at a meeting, talking until time for discussion is exhausted, or simply wearing others down by outtalking them				

a software designer finally decided to make peace with the hardware designer in a telecommunications firm, she asked him to lunch. There, away from their groups—which egged on the conflict—she had the opportunity to discuss cooperation without being branded a pushover or a conspirator. Using the survey as a springboard for conversation, she asked, "Do you think we do some of these things?" After a positive response, she carefully shared a small piece of information that one of her staff had been withholding from his group. At that point she waited to gauge his reaction. If he had flown off the handle she could have aborted the process and still saved face. He didn't. He revealed to her an instance of a hardware design being more flexible than he had led her to believe, and slowly they began to stop playing games, one at a time.

You may want to discuss with the other party or parties the terms of your cooperation. Ensure that you are not seen as a patsy because this could simply escalate the territorial games. Instead, demonstrate the strength and mutual benefits of cooperation, and keep your contingency plan handy in case the other party doesn't reciprocate accordingly.

And remember, someone has to go first.

Belief 2: We pretend we aren't playing territorial games.

Counterproof: We can talk about territorial games.

The reason territoriality has been such a drain on corporate resources is that it has been invisible. We pretend it doesn't exist. When no one talks about it, it is easy to deny and everyone does. Even you. Only when you closely examine your behavior can you see evidence of a territorial drive. Peeling back the cloak of secrecy that surrounds these behaviors isn't easy. Somehow you need to get people to talk about territorial games in order to break through the pretense and the secrecy.

Practice first with one or two people who consider themselves to be on "your side." Build your skills discussing territorial games with friends first. This will help when you approach those who consider you to be the enemy. Understand that most people are unwilling to reveal behaviors that might be emotion-based. Even helping you to identify your territorial games is risky for them. Once they talk about it, they can't help but consider their own behaviors. And unless a crisis demands it, few people are fond of critical self-analysis.

Consider the following comments from individuals participating in the research. Almost everyone interviewed struggled to talk about this aspect of organizational behavior.

> *"I'm having trouble explaining it to you because there's not actual black-and-white stuff. It's intuitive."*

> *"I don't think a third-party observer would observe anything out of the ordinary. It's that covert."*

> *"If you ever get into a group meeting and ask somebody if that's going on, the answer would be 'absolutely not.'"*

> *"The cultural norm that protects this behavior, the reason they get away with it, why they're allowed to do it, is that nobody will admit that it's going on. There's denial that it's really going on."*

One of the reasons others (and you) might be unwilling to discuss territorial games openly is that, once discussed, they are rendered less effective. Laid bare, these games are easily defused. There are itches that people just don't scratch when they are being observed by others. And there are unconscious territorial behaviors that people just don't display when they become conscious of them.

Once you have discussed territorial games, you have put your cards on the table. All cards are open for inspection. The advantage of secrecy is no longer available. The games don't work so well when exposed. This is why people tend to be mindlessly protective of these territorial games. They remove the cloak of secrecy only grudgingly. Instinctively, they know that to discuss these games is to abandon the prospect of using them in blissful ignorance from then on. It is an irreversible process. Once you admit that you are playing territorial games you become sensitized to seeing all of the many games you play. Sometimes it is easier not to know. There is less responsibility to do something about it.

Getting people to talk honestly about territorial games will be a bit of a chore. The good news is that once you do, the behavior change process will already be under way. Real dialogue about territorial games and their detrimental effects is an important behavior change strategy all by itself. Simply admitting that it exists changes the behavior.

One executive, a CFO in a steel company, set up lunch meetings for anyone who wanted to come and talk about territoriality. He was surprised by the number of people who showed up (a lot) and more surprised at the number who spoke up at the meeting (no one). Most of those attending had talked his ear off in the hallway before the group meeting. They were animated and emotional in their personal discussions with him but hated to expose themselves in the group. Why? Once they admitted that territoriality existed in their organization it would be hard to unadmit. No one wanted to go first. And as long as they pretended it didn't exist, they didn't have to do anything about it. A fellow consultant described this as the "steaming turd" syndrome. A group sits around a table on which sits a steaming turd, and then they pretend it isn't there. Because whoever mentions it first has an obligation to remove it and somehow becomes forever associated with steaming turds in everyone's mind. No wonder they don't want to talk about it.

The biggest challenge in laying your groundwork will be creating an atmosphere in which people are ready and willing to discuss their own territorial drives. They are always willing to talk about the territorial games that others play; people are always willing to trash the other guy (as long as he or she isn't in the room). Creating an atmosphere in which people are willing to talk about their own territorial games will be much easier if you can make it seem OK to be territorial.

You can speed up the process if you frame the behaviors as natural and normal. Talking about territorial games can bump up against some powerful self-image concerns. It is much easier to discuss the subject when people don't blame themselves for having the urge. The group needs to treat the territorial drive as a normal aspect of human behavior.

Treating It Like a Natural Survival Urge

The playing of territorial games is a natural human response to a world that is changing at a frightening pace. It is completely understandable. The reframing of territorialism as a natural survival urge enables you to see it without your ego wanting to explain it away.

If we can view territorialism as a behavior from our evolutionary heritage that has outlasted its usefulness, we can skip the time-consuming excuses and rationalizations. That is the main reason I spent so much time building a case for both genetic and cultural imprinting of the territorial urge. If you can get the group to agree that territoriality is just a part of being human, then you are much closer to creating a safe place to discuss it. You can use a nature versus nurture framework as a vehicle to draw people into discussing territoriality.

Treating the playing of territorial games as instinctual makes it a blameless behavior. As a behavioral scientist, I have come to see blame as the enemy of behavior change. As long as people are indulging in blame, they paint themselves as victims and remain powerless. Powerless people can't change. All they can do is sit on their duffs and talk about how terrible everything is. Getting people to talk about territorial behaviors does not mean indulging in a blame session. You may have to let the members of your group vent some frustrations before they are willing to move forward, but try not to let them stay in the blame mode.

The way to move people away from blaming is to position territorial games as a natural survival response that was programmed into our behavior when the world was a simpler place. No blame is attached; you see it as just an old habit that has outlived its usefulness. This is also a good place to use the Territorial Drive survey sheet as a group exercise. Tally up the surveys as a whole and between territories to give the group a starting place from which to discuss all of the games. Once they can talk about it, the next step is to ease group members into a little self-analysis.

Belief 3: "They" are the problem.

Counterproof: You and I are the problem.

Part of the blame stage in changing territorial behaviors means deriding all those Neanderthal turf mongers, office politicians, and sharks out there. It is *always* someone else. It is all those jerks who set up the system who need to change first, right? If they don't change, we can't, right? "I'll tell you who you need to go change, it's Sheri in accounting," or the *other* business unit that has been hogging all the resources or. . . . It's not our fault—we *have* to be territorial because they are. *They* are the problem.

Most groups hold on to this belief until the bitter end. It is usually the last to go. They can buy into the belief that some people don't play territorial games and survive. They can even begin to talk openly about territorial games. But admitting that *they* are part of the problem will take a more powerful experience.

Your first group discussion of territorial games will probably result in a long list of all the external conditions *forcing* them to behave in this manner. Everyone and everything out there are the problem. Not them. They are just trying to survive in the jungle. For most people, this is a core belief with deep roots. Trying to mow this one down without getting to the roots of the belief is as effective as mowing the dandelions in your front lawn. You get to feel successful for about a week.

Remember that people change from the inside out. You need to create an opportunity that will let them decide for themselves that perhaps, just maybe, *they* could be contributing to the territorial games in your organization. I worked with the president of a software company for a year, helping his group make some tough decisions about its future direction that involved abandoning several projects. One was a pet project of his. They didn't have enough resources to fuel all the projects on their agenda and they had to cut something. The first three meetings seemed productive, disarmingly honest, self-analytical, and all ended in clear agreements—none of which were kept. Weak excuses for failing to meet their agreements were met with understanding and tolerance by the president—until the meeting, when he would act irritated. In between meetings, he was invariably the invisible wall or camouflage player who prevented follow-through. Calling him on his behavior in front of the group would have gotten me kicked out of the company. Instead of the direct approach, I used my own version of the Socratic method to get him to acknowledge his territorial drives.

Privately we worked through a series of questions such as, "What is your worst fear if this project is dropped? How might you be keeping this project alive? If you wanted it squashed tomorrow, how would you go about making that happen? What do you achieve by not letting it die?" Eventually, he found it hard to deny that he was contributing to the group's inability to trim the list of projects. Once he admitted this to himself, he was much quicker and more decisive in meetings. He held people to their agreements. As a result, they quickly eliminated the extra projects and reallocated much-needed resources to the core projects they had chosen. Development time was back on track in a month. I doubt that he would have changed had I used the direct approach. The Socratic method allowed him to reach his own conclusions.

The Socratic Method

We are a rebellious lot. The vast majority of us don't take very kindly to someone else telling us "You have a problem." This approach is more likely to generate a belligerent "Oh yeah, buddy? The hell with you" response than the desired "Thank you, please help me change." Use what you know about yourself in designing any intervention for creating change. If *you* don't like to have your faults (games) pointed out to you, others probably don't either.

So how do you point out problems without pointing them out? Easy. Socrates figured this one out a long time ago. When working with groups on territoriality or any other organizational issue, I use my version of the Socratic method. There are four basic principles to follow.

1. *Ask good questions.* Drawing people out slowly with good questions leads them through a guided introspection that can be very revealing without being threatening. Good questions don't attack, but reveal the underlying assumptions behind a statement. Either you are tracing the real reason or challenging their professed reason. You ask questions like: "Did you assume they had a hidden agenda?" "What did you assume it was?" "Did you try to find out more?" "What would have happened if you had assumed they were simply misinformed?" Questions can also shift perceptions to a bigger picture: "What do you think the impact on the organization was?" "Whose job was made more difficult by that action?" Ask questions that provoke introspection.

2. *You reach rather than teach a solution.* Beware of your own psychological territory as the "expert" when you work with others to change territorial behavior. If they sense that you claim the territorial rights to having "the" answer, then your efforts are more likely to generate a miniturf war over who has "the" answer than a useful dialogue about what to do. In order to use the Socratic method you must be nonterritorial about answers and willing to trust the group's ability to eventually see things for themselves.

3. *You appeal to the group's (or individual's) innate ability and desire to reason.* This is difficult. You *have* to believe that the group has the innate ability and desire to reason. Many facilitators allow their frustration with difficult groups to turn into a belief that the group doesn't want to see the problem. Once you believe that they don't *want* to make good choices, you cannot be an effective facilitator.

4. *You train yourself to assume that the reasoning ability is there.* The only problem needing to be addressed is their lack of awareness of how their thinking habits prevent them from seeing the problem. You must allow them to explore their own resistance to seeing it. When I train facilitators, I believe one of the most important skills I can share is the skill of staying silent. If you are babbling on or telling people "what your problem is," then you might as well dig their heels in for them. Artful facilitation means that *they* do the self-analysis, not you.

The Socratic method requires you to be more of a facilitator than a trainer. Trainers tell; facilitators ask. As a facilitator, you act as midwife to the group's insight about its territorial behavior. It is a good idea to set up a series of ground rules for this sort of process so that things don't break down when it gets uncomfortable. The following list is a sample from a group that designed its own ground rules. I strongly recommend allowing the group to choose its own ground rules. Groups usually choose great ground rules and are more likely to follow ones they have designed themselves than any you might impose.

Ground Rules for Dialogue About Territoriality

1. Don't jump to conclusions.
2. Blame territorial instincts, not people.
3. Ensure that no one feels attacked.
4. Avoid generalizations.
5. Embrace the "irrational" as well as the rational.
6. Respect each individual's perspective.
7. Try to see it from his or her point of view.

After presenting descriptions of the territorial games (the chart in Figure 3 makes a good overhead), ask people where they have seen such behaviors before. Allow some time for blame talk. This gives people the opportunity to vent their pent-up frustrations.

Give them time to explore the concept of territoriality as a natural survival urge. Establish the concept that everyone plays territorial games. Once people begin to feel comfortable, ask them to identify the games that they play most often. This is something of a trick question. You may have noticed that no-where in the process have you given anyone the opportunity to say that they don't play territorial games. If you are genuine in your approach, if you lead the way by admitting *your* games, then they will either not notice the omission or not mind it.

The Socratic method works so well with territoriality because it allows people access to their innate reason. Because the facilitator never tries to impose a conclusion, people are willing to see conclusions for themselves. If you are careful not to craft your questions to appear as accusations, the group will usually respond with candor and self-disclosure. You may want to use the self-tests at the end of each chapter in Part Two to stimulate more dialogue. I definitely recommend using the chart in Figure 3 as a group exercise. When you share the results with the group, ask open-ended questions, like:

> "What price do you think we pay when we play territorial games?"
> "When someone is being territorial with you, how does it affect your productivity?"
> "How do you feel at the end of the day when you have been involved in one of these games?"
> "Which games seem more like smart business moves than games?"

You can think up more questions, but the purpose is to generate introspection that will result in group members' acknowledgment of their complicity in creating an environment of territoriality. Seeing that they are part of the problem is the final wall that needs to be torn down before you can build new behaviors.

Once you have a critical mass of people who are ready to consider that

- they don't have to play territorial games,
- this is something they can talk about, and
- it is up to them to change it,

you have laid the groundwork for implementing change.

17

Building a New Map

"The great French Marshal Lyautey once asked his gardener to plant a tree. The gardener objected that the tree was slow growing and would not reach maturity for 100 years. The Marshal replied, 'In that case, there is no time to lose; plant it this afternoon.'"

—J. F. Kennedy

You have torn down the old walls, ripped up the foundations of the old territorial games, and now you can start afresh. Once the beliefs that held old maps in place are loosened a bit, you must immediately build new beliefs and new behaviors. If you don't, the old ones will come back or new ones will evolve by default. Rather than trust that new lines of territory will evolve along the boundaries you desire, you can consciously build a new map of a larger, more cooperative territory. With new maps and new perceptions, new behaviors will follow.

Behavior change doesn't mean that you change people. People don't change. No matter what you do, people still have emotions of fear, anger, and desire. They are still concerned about their psychological survival and want to claim enough territory to feel safe. They still repeat patterns of behavior. But now that you know all this, you can redirect these territorial dynamics to work *for* the organization instead of against it.

People don't change, but they *can* change their patterns of behavior when their perceptions of territory change. This happens on several levels: personal, work group, and organizational environment. Shifting each of these perceptual realities means building new maps with new lines of territory.

Drawing a Bigger Map

Lines of territory usually stop where the information and communication stop. There is an old story that was told by William Oncken, Jr., a naval officer in World War II, which gives us an example of how information and communication can transform small maps into bigger maps. Back then, destroyers had a maximum speed of 20 knots—except for one particular destroyer, which was commanded by Admiral Arleigh Burke. Apparently his destroyer could go an extra 5 knots over and above the supposed maximum speed. How his engine room managed to perform over and above the rest of the fleet was the subject of wide speculation.

Folklore has it that the admiral realized that the engine room, 24 feet below the waterline, was cut off from all the action. Topside staff could hear artillery fire, see planes fighting, and experience the mission of the ship, firsthand. But below, shut off from any noise except demands for more power, the guys of the engine room staff felt that they wouldn't be missed even if they didn't show up for chow. They didn't feel a part of the action. To remedy this, Admiral Burke wired the entire ship with a PA system over which was broadcast a blow-by-blow sportscast of everything that happened topside, complete with live sound effects. After that, when the engine room got a request for more power, the men knew why, they cared more, and they felt a part of the action. They had a bigger picture because they had more information.

As you consciously prepare to construct new, more inclusive perceptions of turf that will replace old narrow ones, you may want to remember Admiral Burke. Films, lectures, and mission statements could never have changed the engine room's perception of territory as much as the experience of being directly involved and realizing its importance to the mission did. This sort of experience forges a clearer perception of personal territory and a sense of control over one's psychological survival prospects.

Finding New Ways to Feed
Psychological Survival Needs

People need to feel that they understand their survival situation. They want to feel important to the decision makers, important enough to be kept informed. Those guys in the engine room needed to feel a connection to the rest of the ship. Their response to feeling left out was less commitment to the mission. People in your organization act the same way. When they don't feel that they're being informed, when they don't feel important, they start playing games. Their psychological survival is threatened. They may even see the organization as the enemy.

Some people think that how "important" an individual feels is "not my problem." It's not—if you don't have anyone withholding information from you, deliberately going slow on a project, or impeding the progress of an innovation. But if you do, and you want to decrease territorial games, then it *is* your problem. Many people in organizations today feel as if they have a postage-stamp–size piece of psychological territory that wouldn't be missed if they got run over by a bus.

You can't expect people to drop their defenses (territorial games) when they feel left out or expendable. Everyone is feeling expendable these days . . . because they (and you) are. Even the current high rates of employment have not dispelled dismal perceptions of job security. This is because downsizing and re-engineering have institutionalized expendability. It is a new fact of life and we need to stop pretending it isn't. Denying it or refusing to talk about it only creates a vacuum of information that invites the survival mind's worst-case scenario. In that worst-case scenario, the psychological survival of the uninformed feels threatened and they will "protect" themselves by making territorial moves. To counteract this worst-case scenario response, people need enough information to develop confidence in their ability to survive the changes.

One way is to share more information about the changes—to build something like Admiral Burke's PA system. The secretive manner in which companies are organizing and reorganizing their internal structures only contributes to people's fears. For some, it is worse than being in the bowels of the engine room. A new job definition every two weeks wreaks havoc with territorial perceptions. When people know they can't expect to have the same job in another two years and don't know when, where, or how they will pay the mortgage after that, they experience chronic levels of anxiety that contribute to territorial games. Nothing short of a safer, more empowered view of the future will change that dynamic. Since no organization can afford to promise lifetime employment anymore, organizations need to find other ways to feed employees' psychological survival needs—or, more precisely, allow them to feed their own needs.

Tricking people into feeling they aren't expendable, when they *are*, doesn't work. People aren't dumb. They can figure it out. This sort of insincerity breeds distrust and more territorial games at the individual level. Apathy or resentment replaces motivation and productivity. On the other hand, treating employees like important contributors who *can handle the truth* feeds psychological survival needs.

This is not about coddling employees or initiating silly self-esteem programs. Treat people like adults and they are more likely to act like adults and solve their own problems. With enough information, adults will take responsibility for feeding their own psychological survival needs.

Giving Them Lots of Information

I often hear the accusation, "They want me to solve their problems for them." Is it any wonder, when most managers don't pass on enough information for employees to solve their own problems. A manager can be so caught up in her own territorial game of information manipulation that she doesn't realize she is drawing a territorial line between herself and her staff.

Many employees are in a constant state of fear because they don't have enough information to make good decisions. In a vacuum, people inevitably construct the worst-case scenario. They feel dependent, vulnerable. Vulnerable enough to play territorial games. Our organizational cultures have trained people to take directions rather than to take charge. Their psychological survival has been wired to depend on the organization for recognition and appreciation. The organization is not meeting their needs, so they play territorial games to make themselves feel more safe and secure.

As long as organizations play the information manipulation game with their own employees they can expect to see other territorial games played in return. However, given enough information, individuals can rewire themselves to be more independent and confident about their survival.

Giving people plenty of information accomplishes three things. First, it sends a message about where the territorial lines are drawn (they are "in" rather than "out"). Second, it generates feelings of importance, because they have been trusted with valuable information. Third, it empowers them to take care of themselves. You *want* people to take care of themselves. That way, you don't have to. You can focus on the work.

Some managers think that self-interest is inconsistent with the good of the organization. Not true. Organizations *depend* on self-interest. You just have to ensure that self-interest is tied to the good of the organization. When employees can achieve their own psychological survival goals by making the organization successful, then you both win. At this point, organizational territory becomes personal territory. They use a bigger map.

One medium-size manufacturing company discovered that sharing even negative information can decrease fear levels. Industry downturns and decreasing sales had made employees fearful of losing their jobs. Without clear information, they constructed their own worst-case scenarios. (Remember, the survival mind is programmed to overreact rather than to underreact.) Teamwork diminished as workers competed with each other for visibility and shirked risk taking. For a variety of reasons this company decided to implement open-book accounting. It was prepared to do damage control on morale once everyone had the facts.

There was no need for damage control. Morale actually improved. Sure, the news was bad, but it wasn't as bad as the rumors that had been floating around when everyone was left guessing. The sharing of information galvanized the group into a "we can survive this" collective and improved performance within six months. When an organization chooses to share vital information with workers, the impact can be powerful.

Ignoring the fact that people are primarily driven by self-interest is bad for an organization. Companies that ignore (or compete with) self-interest try to get more from their people for less and less until they inadvertently increase the territorial games in their organization. They unwittingly draw lines of territory between employer and employee. By denying employees their self-interests (personal territory), they only cause the employees to focus more on protecting and grabbing territory to feed denied self-interests. Organizations that do this cross the line of diminishing returns. Rather than increasing productivity, they generate even more internal lines of division that breed destructive territorial games.

Only when the organizational processes and goals help feed self-interest and psychological survival needs will people shift their focus from territorial games to organizational goals. Sharing plenty of information gives employees more choices and more opportunities to link self-interest to the organizational good. When the organizational win means their win, people begin to feel like part of one unified territory instead of like outsiders.

Once this personal level of inclusion is created, there are other ways to create feelings of inclusion across the organization. Ensuring that all members of the organization share a common vision will build feelings of inclusion across old territorial lines.

Creating the Experience of a Unified Organization Territory

Since the territory we are discussing here is intangible, then the illusion of territory is totally susceptible to perception. The bad news is that you can't see, touch, or feel a perception. The good news is that since it is not a physical reality, you can create it however you want. Creating the perception of inclusion and interdependence is much easier if people believe that they are all working toward the same goals and vision.

Your organization may have physical grounds, a factory, offices, and so on, but people can still feel as if they don't belong— even when they spend most of their waking hours there. Just because people are employees of the same organization doesn't mean that they are all on the same team. Perceptions of a collective, cooperative, unified territory are unlikely to occur spontaneously. You must consciously construct this perception.

The most damaging territorial maneuvering operates between factions that reside within the same organization—the us-and-them of two departments competing for the same budget, geographically separate divisions that sabotage each other, gender or racially divided groups caught up in their differences. Only creating an experience of being on the same team will override subterritorial impulses with a higher-order survival need: the survival of the organization. It is only *experience* that can create this perception. Telling people about their mutual survival situation won't cut it.

In a recent situation, I was called in to work with a construction company that was already one year behind schedule on a five-year job. The job was unusual in that both steel and concrete were equally important. Most of the time one or the other ends up as top dog on a job and it then calls most of the shots. It may not be fair, but it is functional.

In this situation, both were equally important and a turf war had developed. To make matters worse, the head steel guy and the head concrete guy had engaged in a running personal feud for over ten years. By the time I got there they were hiding cranes from each other (in a big city this actually *is* possible) and the site trailer door was mangled with kick marks as one or the other stormed out after yet another shouting match. In this environment, I would have been foolish to talk about how "we all need to work together." They knew they were behind schedule. They knew that infighting was making things worse. Their potential for hefty bonuses was dwindling daily. There was every logical reason for them to call a truce, and yet they hadn't. Because when emotions are involved, logical or rational explanations cannot penetrate the emotional brain deeply enough to change perceptions.

I had to create an experience that would override their perceptions of division. First, I did all the things discussed in Chapters 15 and 16. After laying the groundwork, we took ten key players to an off-site two-day retreat. We did lots of sophisticated psychological stuff, but to my surprise, the most powerful experience was a simple game. The game required high levels of teamwork and accelerated information flow. These guys aced it. To this day, I have never seen any team perform so well at this particular game. They blew it away, and the best part was they *knew* they had. There were high fives and back slaps all around. The team had rediscovered what it felt like to work together. They experienced the extraordinary level of competence waiting to be tapped in this crack team of construction professionals. The emotional high of the weekend wore off, but no one on that team forgot how it felt to work together. They had proven to themselves (and their survival minds) that it could be done. Six months later, they aren't quite on schedule, but they are well on their way.

Memos about an organization's vision can't create an emotional experience. Circulated mission statements or purpose statements posted on the walls will not permeate minds well enough to translate to feelings. The emotional brain responds to experience, not rhetoric.

Experiencing the Need for Group Survival

The experience that you want to create will demonstrate to employees that they are members of one inclusive territory contributing to a collective survival. Even if you could, you wouldn't want to eliminate territoriality. It is a powerful motivating force. You don't want to stop it, you want to tap into it. Think of the energy now flowing into territorial games as being available for your organization's goals.

Territoriality can work *for* the organization. Much of the time it does. We collaborate in organizations in a modern-day replica of hunters choosing to survive in groups rather than alone. One problem is that our groups have gotten much larger than our internal territorial programs are designed to protect. How can we identify as a member of a territory with members numbering in the hundreds, thousands, or tens of thousands? It's too big. So people break it down, draw their lines around fifteen cubicles and act as if those fifteen people are the tribe. Smaller organizations may not have the problems of scale, but they still subdivide themselves as a natural reaction to the inter-

nal conflicts that inevitably occur in business. Without a constant reminder/experience that you are all on the same team,
your team will begin to divide.

In order to build a new map with the entire organization as
one unified territory, people need to have a series of experiences
that proves their perceptions of division to be false. Most team
building is designed to accomplish this. People who normally
don't spend enough time together are brought together to experience each other as teammates instead of rivals.

Using "Territory Building" as an Experience

The term *team building* carries a lot of baggage. Too many people
have experienced team building that was a waste of time. In
order to differentiate our discussion I use the terms *team building*
and *territory building* interchangeably. Territory building is the
purpose of most team building anyway. Consider your past experience with any team-building activity that you would label
worthwhile. What did you get out of it? What was the purpose?
In most situations, the purpose was to reduce internal lines of
division, misunderstandings resulting from conflicts, and to
build a feeling of team so strong that continuing feelings of inclusion would override internal conflicts of interest.

Territory building can be accomplished in many ways. One
company organizes a weekend trip for the entire organization
once a year. The excitement of planning the trip, the experience
of the trip, the inclusiveness of playing together as one group
build experiences of team that are so strong they can help override internal business conflicts that occur during the year. The
reduction in internal territorial games is worth every penny the
company spends on this trip.

Any activity that builds bridges instead of highlighting differences can be used to accomplish territory building. One of the
most common objections to an investment in team building is
that these sessions don't seem to be addressing relevant business
problems. That is because most relevant business problems *generate* internal conflicts. (If there is no conflict, it isn't a problem.)
Expecting a team-building session to focus on an internal
conflict only highlights the internal boundaries you want to

override. Team building needs to highlight similarities, not differences. And if a Christmas party is the only vehicle through which people can experience their similarities, then that's better than nothing.

Learning games, simulations, and other group activities can build feelings of territory across old divisive lines. It doesn't matter which activity you choose. As long as it highlights the experience of being on one collective team, even rafting down a river can build experiences of inclusion that will permeate the group's emotional experience of territory. In fact, the more emotion generated in whatever activity you choose, the longer the territory-building effects will last. That is why outdoor team building with physical risks and trust-building exercises works so well. The emotions experienced together as an interdependent team cement feelings of inclusion. Emotions act like superglue for memory. Build emotion into an experience and it lasts longer in memory, has more weight in perceptions, and exercises a stronger influence over future behaviors.

Territory building *can* be orchestrated around business issues. With a trained facilitator you can even tackle deep internal conflicts and tap into emotional issues in a way that forges connections instead of highlights division. Open-space processes described by Harrison Owen in *Open Space Technology: A User's Guide* offer a wonderful format that can be used for strategic planning and other business issues. However, if you aren't confident that your facilitation skills can manage the conflicts, it is a better idea to use nonbusiness-related activities to build feelings of inclusion. The one exception is the activity of building organizational vision. Done properly, this exercise can create a strong experience of inclusion across the entire organization *and* address an important business issue.

Using Vision as an Experience

Collective vision drives to the very essence of a single unified organizational territory. Hunters and gatherers didn't need to spend a day generating a collective vision. They shared a pretty simple one: food and shelter. It just sort of occurred to them when they woke up in the morning. "I'm hungry, you look hungry, let's work together." Nowadays we need to give a little more attention to vision if only because of the exponential number of choices involved. If we are going to share a single cause, we have to use some kind of process to bring it all together.

After experiencing a little more internal turmoil than usual, a nearby university asked me to facilitate a vision retreat for an academic department. University professors are by nature individual achievers. I realized that facilitating a group vision was going to be like trying to herd cats. Each professor viewed his field of research as so specialized that he rarely looked for common ground with anyone else. One of the first comments of the day was, "I don't see any advantage in a group vision and I think this is a waste of time." Yes, well, on this enthusiastic note we began the process of articulating individual visions (a first step in creating a collective vision). Jaws dropped as one by one they discovered the overlap of some of their research. They found that they were duplicating efforts in several areas and that, with a little effort, their limited resources could be made to go much further.

Before that day, several members of the faculty had spent much of their time and effort positioning themselves to grab at the limited resources available. Every time one of them left his office, the head of the department must have felt like a piñata. However, after exploring their collective vision they experienced the department as a unified territory. In the next few months, five professors collaborated on a successful grant proposal that incorporated six different research projects into a budget that was less than half the size of the six previously separate proposals. I want to believe that the cooperation demonstrated by the collaborative approach had a lot to do with the success of their grant proposal.

There has been enough written about the process of creating an organizational vision. It is not necessary to duplicate those efforts here. However, when considering vision in terms of human territorial drive there are certain guidelines that will help you to use organization vision making as a unifying experience to decrease internal territorial games. The first thing to remember is to ensure that as many people as possible participate.

If vision is genuinely developed through a collective effort, employees get the opportunity to experience collaboration across internal lines. Be warned that "genuinely developed through a collective effort" means that everyone contributes. It is messier, takes longer, and can turn out differently than you expected. But you will have created a shared experience of organizational unity that can forge collaboration in a way that a vision statement posted on the wall will never accomplish.

In order to use vision to develop inclusive territorial boundaries, you must ensure that your vision process is a true collaboration rather than the more typical us/them experience of a vision handed down from on high. When people struggle with the big issues together, smaller internal conflicts shrink to their proper size. Allowing everyone (or at least a cross-sectional representation of your organization) to participate in crafting the organization's vision builds the experience of "being in this together." The end result is usually not quite so elegant, is less carefully crafted, and may even be flawed, but it belongs to everyone and is ten times more powerful than a perfectly crafted vision statement hanging on a wall. The vision process is a perfect vehicle for building organizational experiences that create feelings of inclusion.

One senior executive whose success in a newly merged organization depended on eliminating old territorial boundaries found that a powerful group vision helped him override subterritorial boundaries:

> *"If you understand the vision and the purpose in what you are trying to create, then there are some boundaries that become common boundaries. The danger in there is the assumption that you and I both understand the vision. That we are both operating by the same set of rules and that isn't true. Boundaries need to be articulated. Vision accomplishes that."*

Assuming that everyone understands organizational boundaries and organizational vision is as bad as not having one. There is a world of difference between a leader who has an organizational vision (with clear boundaries) and an organization that embraces the vision. Simply telling people about your organizational vision does not create an experience that embeds that vision in their hearts. Vision requires more than a memo.

Again, the catch in allowing vision to be a true collaboration is that the vision may not turn out to be what you intended. That is a risk you take. Of course, forcing a vision down their throats won't turn out to be what you intended either. The balance in allowing true collaboration and keeping your group's vision on track is to ensure that the group has enough information to reach the same conclusions you reached about appropriate organizational direction. This is where a trained facilitator is useful. When everyone does reach the same conclusions about direction, the effect on internal territorial games is profound.

Using Company Structure and Policy as an Experience

A common vision can override many territorial games, but if organizational structure pits people against each other in territorial battles over resources and rewards, you've still got a problem. Even a collective organizational vision cannot overcome divisive internal policies and structure. Look at the territorial map you drew of your organization. Highlight the areas where most territorial games occur and consider what internal structural elements may contribute to these territorial games. Frequently, overly competitive reward structures, resource allocation processes, or information handling procedures are to blame for destructive infighting.

Estrangement by Performance Review

With the best of intentions, many managers set up internal "friendly competitions" that incite all-out turf wars. The public display of individual sales figures can build healthy competition, but a single bonus awarded to the highest performer can generate territorial games. Any internal boundaries that display high levels of territorial games should be analyzed in terms of structures or policies that may be contributing to the problem.

Are your policies, procedures, or structures divisive or unifying? Performance review systems that result in a certain percentage of individual winners and losers can generate internal battles. This sort of reward structure can build a group of individual achievers who may easily withhold information from each other, discredit peers, or otherwise inhibit their colleagues' success. If that is the case in your organization, you may want to reconsider redesigning the performance review system to be more inclusive.

Working with a medium-size retail company, I discovered that redesigning the performance review system can provide double payoffs in decreasing territorial games. In this company the two largest stores had built walls of division between them. You were either a member of "North" or "South." Another line of division existed between the brothers who owned the company and their employees. Every perception of role, responsibility, and task was heavily influenced by some "us-and-them" perception. The brothers wanted employees to take on more "ownership," but the existing performance review system only contributed to dysfunctional lines of division.

The first problem was that the existing performance review form had been designed by the brothers and handed down. The second problem was that the described roles and responsibilities did not reflect interdependence and perpetuated competition between North and South. We decided not only to redesign the system but also to use the redesigning process itself to build perceptions of inclusion. The process we used began with a collective vision process, incorporating the expectations of peers and subordinates (not just bosses) to define roles, and was collaboratively developed with those who would be reviewed. Each step required so much interaction across old territorial lines that these experiences began to erase old perceptions of separation. By the time we finished designing the new performance review system, employees on all levels had articulated too many other important things (like organizational vision and cooperation) to worry about who was North and who was South.

Promoting collective wins as well as individual wins can provide needed balance. Finding the balance between healthy competition and unhealthy infighting isn't easy. The motivation to "win" is a strong one and tapping into it can generate a lot of momentum. On the other hand, territorial games and infighting can do a lot of damage. You must determine whether territorial games are taking your organization three steps back for every two steps forward. If so, redesigning your performance review system or reward structure can decrease territorial games.

Resource Battles

Resource allocation is another area where organizational structure and policies can contribute to territorial games. There is no way around the fact that, in any organization, individuals and groups compete with each other for limited resources. People get attached to their own ideas, they see things from their own vantage point, and even if they subscribe to the same organizational vision, they have different opinions about how to get there. If your budget process or strategic planning sessions exacerbate these differences, you will only stimulate divisive territorial games that sabotage collective reasoning.

Closed sessions, blind submissions, and decisions made by one individual instead of a group emphasize internal lines of division. At the moment, it may *feel* more efficient to make decisions by reducing the involvement of others and tightening information flow, but, ultimately, even good decisions can be sabotaged by the territorial games of the uninvolved.

Use a decision-making process that includes the collaboration of both those who receive the resources and those who relinquish the resources. It may take longer to reach a decision, but in the end you will have reached a stable decision that is not sabotaged by ongoing territorial games. When internally opposed groups are forced to find a higher-order solution among themselves, they are more likely to live peacefully with it than if they are subjected to an imposed solution. The extra time spent will be well worth it.

Information Distribution

Finally, the way that information is distributed will either increase feelings of inclusion or increase feelings of exclusion. If information is allocated on a need-to-know basis, consider who is making that decision and how you can protect the process from that individual's territorial drives. Sometimes sensitive information needs to be withheld, but my experience suggests that territorial impulses operate to label information "sensitive" more often than is necessary. Information is the most valuable territory in our organizations today. Making sure that information gatekeepers are well acquainted with their own territorial drives can help them to monitor their own tendencies to play games with information. Building information forums with multiple access points can neutralize territorial games over information.

Technology gives us an incredible vehicle for sharing information. Like anything, it can be abused. Since flooding people with too much information can achieve the same effects as withholding information, you must protect against the possible malicious obedience of an information gatekeeper. With sane solutions, information technology can build strong links and feelings of inclusion across the entire organization.

This is not to suggest that company policies and structure need to promote feelings of inclusion no matter what. Your policies and structure need to make good business sense. They also need to unify your organization rather than divide it. Consider your internal policies for their compound effects on organizational performance. If they are doing more harm than good, change them. If you can't change them, then you will need to ensure that external lines of territory are clear enough to override these unavoidable internal conflicts. When internal conflicts are unavoidably running high, what you need is an enemy!

Redefining the Enemy

If two internal factions are treating each other like the enemy, then it is time to stage an alien invasion. Bringing in some Godzilla-like enemy will help clarify the real lines of defense. Drawing bold territorial lines *around* your organization that override the ones within the organization will not only decrease internal territorial games but will also tap into a powerful motivating force. Redefining the enemy can energize group efforts to be more competitive in the appropriate directions.

If people need an enemy (and they do), give them one. You can redirect the fear, anger, and desire that were running along internal boundaries and transfer them to external boundaries. I am *not* promoting the artificial stimulation of more fear or anger.

Scare tactics backfire. Both fear and anger (and desire for that matter) are very distracting emotions in high doses. Excessive amounts of these emotions only cloud thinking and spill over into inappropriate areas.

Still, the transfer of our natural territorial instincts from internal "enemies" to external "enemies" is a better use of the territorial drive than infighting. Admiral Burke's PA system focused the engine room on the *real* enemy instead of on the jerks topside who ceaselessly demanded more power and were never satisfied. In such a stressful situation it is much better to be territorial about our company as a whole than about our particular division against our own people.

In order to influence territorial games, you must influence where the territorial lines are drawn. Since you will never eliminate territorial lines, why not put them where you want them?

Remember that territorial behaviors are based in survival instincts. You are territorial to protect what is "yours" from someone or something . . . from the enemy. But who is the enemy in this make-believe battle over psychological survival? It depends. The enemy depends on the territory. And the territory depends on the enemy. Siblings who fight, squabble, and tear each other apart when alone will pull together to fight side by side and protect each other when threatened by the neighborhood bully. A common enemy unifies an otherwise diverse group.

It is not necessary to manufacture illusions of threat. There are enough real threats facing any organization to provide the necessary external focus. All you need to do is shine a spotlight (or design a PA system) that highlights the real threats that exist. A bright, clear picture of an organization's enemy can be enough to greatly decrease turf wars and infighting.

One of my favorite business books to hit the market recently is *How to Drive Your Competition Crazy* by Guy Kawasaki. Beginning with his Apple versus IBM experience, Kawasaki has developed a how-to manual for exploiting the drive and passion that can come from spotlighting an external enemy. In the chapter titled "Know Thy Enemy" he gives a variety of methods for snooping out, analyzing, and exploiting the weaknesses of the competition. Each step is designed to incite a sense of competition, to stimulate a "we can do better than that" reaction. Focusing on a big bad enemy can give a company the kind of energy and commitment that David used to slay Goliath. It will also diminish squabbles behind the lines.

Without refocusing, people will naturally pay more attention to daily conflicts than to bigger-picture conflicts. In order to compete with the daily experiences of internal "enemies," you must create a powerful experience that can divert attention to an external enemy. Even if there are several to choose from, it is a good idea to choose only one or two "enemies" for specific focus. General references to vaguely defined threats don't grab the emotional mind enough to compete with the daily irritations that drive a wedge between peers. You need to give the enemy a name and a face.

Painting the Competition as the Enemy

GM and Ford use each other as unifying enemies. Microsoft uses IBM. MCI uses AT&T. Fighting a competitor creates more cohesion for a group. Even if group members disagree about which software feature to develop first, they can agree who the enemy is.

Don't assume that your employees see the same enemy you see. You may think it is obvious that XYZ company is your enemy, but if you don't spend time and effort building that perception within your production group, they may continue to see marketing as the enemy. Since perceptions are built from experience, you need to generate a series of experiences that focus territorial defenses against your chosen competitor.

When building perceptions, use of a series of five one-minute experiences over time will be more effective than one five-minute experience. *That is one of the most important and useful principles I have ever learned.* Let me repeat it: When building perceptions, a series of five one-minute experiences over time are more effective than one five-minute experience. Frequency over time compounds the effect. Remember, you are competing with the daily experiences of internal conflicts. Redefining the enemy as an outside competitor means overriding the frequency or intensity of these daily experiences with reminders of the external conflicts facing your organization.

To create these series of one-minute experiences, some companies circulate sales statistics that monitor the organization's position relative to its competitors. Wins are enthusiastically celebrated and losses somberly analyzed. Others use company conferences to study, identify, and even vilify the competition. Derogatory names and a little competition bashing don't hurt. Think about how football teams build rivalries. Giving the competitor horns and a tail is a harmless enough way to redirect internal antagonisms. Just keep it private—you are playing an intentional territorial game here, so don't forget that it works better when it stays beneath the surface.

Any solution must dramatically affect the perceptions of the entire organization so that you all feel you are on the same side. We need to know who "us" is and who "them" is. We need this knowledge so much that we will invent lines of division to satisfy that need. You might as well tap into this need for an enemy by consistently and frequently pointing to a worthwhile competitor. Tell people who "them" is. Show them who "them" is. Remind them often who "them" is and they are much more likely to behave like a unified "us."

The enemy doesn't have to be outside the organization. For many reasons you may choose not to focus on an external competitor as the enemy. With global organizations, partnering arrangements, and co-opetition, your competition today may be your partner tomorrow. Perhaps you can't afford the luxury of an external enemy. In these situations, you need a more abstract enemy. Any negative patterns or bad habits, the missing of deadlines, or falling behind in new product development can become the enemy. Using the same principles of frequent and consistent focus will help you to shift attention away from internal conflicts to a common defense. You may even want to make territorial games the enemy.

Territorial Games as the Enemy

When the enemy can be articulated as territoriality itself, a group can be unified in its efforts to counteract this primitive instinct in its own organization. Pogo said, "I have seen the enemy and he is us." Positioning territorial games as the enemy has several advantages. When an entire organization works together to defeat the effects of irrational territorial games, people not only have a common goal that overrides territorial games; their common goal *is* to override territorial games. When the organization's vision is already clear, highlighting territorial games as the enemy of organizational vision operates to bring groups together and to erase internal lines of division.

There are several principles to follow when designing your process. First, ensure that the focus is temporary. The effects, of course, will last long after the focus. But your focus on territorial games as the enemy needs to have a clear beginning, middle, and end. Too many organizational behavior change initiatives lose their power because the organizers don't know when to quit. Overworking a concept can desensitize employees to its value. I call it the nagging effect. Nagging people often enough just builds their skills in tuning you out. To avoid this effect, make it clear from the beginning that, while you hope to achieve lasting effects, the focus will be temporary. If you need to, you can repeat the process again five years from now. But for now, keep it brief.

A twelve-month period for the process works well. Twelve months is enough time to initiate lasting behavior change and short enough to avoid fatigue. Do your groundwork as described in Chapter 16 and build a shared perception of the destructive nature of territorial games. This is easier with hard data. I use an anonymous companywide survey that measures the destructive effects of territorial games. Hard statistics and anonymous quotes help stir things up a bit and disrupt old patterns and beliefs. You can design your own survey or use the survey in Figure 3. Once territorial games have been established as the enemy, all you need do is maintain the focus. Some sort of monthly communication, preferably facilitated follow-up sessions, will keep people vigilant against the enemy of territorial games.

Design your intervention to include a measure at the end of the twelve-month period to evaluate your progress. Use the same survey again to measure the decrease in territorial games. An end goal concentrates the group's focus on decreasing territorial games. It also provides you with an objective measurement that evaluates the effects of your efforts.

If you are going to spend the time and effort to decrease territorial games, you might as well use the opportunity to instill new games to replace the old ones. Replacing old behaviors with new ones prevents the old ones from creeping back. Besides, what are people going to do with all the extra time they *used* to spend playing territorial games?

18

Playing New Games

"Help thy brother's boat across and lo! thine own has reached the shore."

—Hindu proverb

Aristotle called us political animals. He categorized the political instinct right up there with the instinct to reproduce. I think we have enough evidence since then to agree with him. Using the term *territorial drive* is just another way to talk about politics. We are innately motivated to own, control, and protect. As long as there are scarce resources we will compete for dominance over those resources.

New Games to Replace the Old Ones

Fighting a human instinct is an uphill battle. I don't recommend it. I think it is a better idea to find a way to ride the instinct and use its power. If we are going to play political games, why not choose healthy ones? We *enjoy* games of power and territory, strategy and finesse. Recognizing this human need means that we can design new, more positive games to replace the old ones.

A game is just a repetitive pattern of behavior. A game is a habit, if you will. If you accept that we are pattern-repeating organisms, then you will want to choose the patterns you repeat rather than let them choose you. Designing new habits and giving them game names is a self-management tool that can help you and your group direct behavior patterns in the direction you desire. If you make no conscious effort, your behavior will probably drift toward the unconscious automatic directions chosen by your territorial drives.

Below are two alternatives to territorial games that you can use to increase your options the next time you feel an emotional impulse to play one of your old games. Introduce these games or, better yet, have your group design its own games as its chosen alternatives to destructive territorial maneuvering. Focusing on these new games gives the emotional mind a better menu to choose from the next time things get tense.

The Trust-Building Game

It is fascinating to observe a group develop its own definition for the trust-building game. They reach deep into old issues and beneath the surface of current issues. They grapple over a common definition of what is fair and right. Trust depends on having the same definition of what is fair and what is right. The group needs to ask itself what "fair" really means. Does fair mean that rewards reflect effort or productive contribution, or should all share equally? Are promotional decisions based on seniority or merit? When is it right to withhold information? If group members are being genuine, a group's struggle to articulate what trust means in terms of behavior will automatically build bridges across old lines of division.

The experiences that previously built distrust and divided groups into factions occurred because of opposing perceptions of what was "right." Trust means that we share the same view and can count on each other to share that same view tomorrow as well as today. Trust means that we are on the same side, protecting the same territory, using the same rules.

You have your own definition of trust building. I have mine. And both are useless to any group until it has struggled a bit to define its own. When bringing a group together to choose new games, it is imperative that group members define the game, not you. A group will play a game of its own invention with much more enthusiasm than it will play your game or my game.

One group I worked with spent a full day defining its version of the trust-building game. Many people would consider this a waste of time. After all, at the end of the day, all they had to show for their efforts was a list of good intentions. But it wasn't the list that created the behavior change. It was the process of revealing to each other how they felt about trust and making agreements with each other. Over the next year their behavior and their language showed the effects of this discussion.

They had decided that their trust-building game would be played by (1) assuming the positive intent of others, (2) keeping agreements or advising others of problems asap, and (3) casting no silent vetos (i.e., speaking up if they disagreed). After that day they used shorthand references like "I'm not seeing positive intent here" to remind each other of their agreements. They caught themselves more often in behaviors that might break trust and corrected them sooner. And they were more proactive in trust building because they had elevated the new game to the level of a goal that was just as important as meeting deadlines.

The best way to guide a group in defining its own games is through examples. Tell your own stories about how the trust-building game might play out. Ask group members to share their ideas too. One example I share concerns one of the individuals in the example. He had an incredible wit. Because he was so funny, his sarcasm often relieved the tensions of the group with giggles and guffaws—except that the person he had just ridiculed usually wasn't laughing. I wish I could report that after the group had decided to play the trust-building game, the sarcastic comments stopped. Well they didn't, but the targets of his jokes used rule #1 to lessen the sting and laugh along with the rest of the group. Make up your own stories and get others to give some examples about how the trust-building game might play out.

People who play the trust-building game are building bridges for the future. It can be a fun game. Trust building can result from making and keeping small agreements. It works even when the agreements aren't very important because it is an *experience.* If another department has been the enemy, playing the trust-building game may mean promising it a report for Monday at 9:00 A.M. and delivering it exactly at 9:00 A.M. on Monday. It can be played by suggesting a meeting to discuss a sensitive issue and making sure the meeting happens. Any kept agreement is a part of the trust-building game. If you need to make the agreements small in order to be sure you can keep them, then do so.

Playing this game even once a day will go a long way toward overcoming internal lines of territory and building inclusive perceptions of one unified organizational turf.

The Community-Building Game

Territory requires trust, but that isn't enough. There is an intangible element of shared territory that can be called "community." When everyone in an organization feels that they are part of the same community, information flows freely and problems are more likely to be solved collaboratively than adversarially. But what is community? And how do you play the community-building game? Again, any definition presented here is of limited use to you or your group. You need to come up with your own definition of the community-building game.

One method is to explore what you know about creating community in a neighborhood and transfer that to the business environment. Taking a pie to a new neighbor can translate into sending a welcome e-mail to a new employee. Mowing your neighbor's lawn at the same time you do your own may translate into picking up extra copies of the new benefits package to deliver to workmates. There are no recipes for community building. Everyone plays it differently. Playing the community-building game may mean sending preliminary designs to a geographically remote division for its input before the designs are finalized.

Some community-building efforts translate directly: remembering the names of someone's children, acknowledging their success with a card or memo. Helping them meet their own goals, acknowledging their contributions, and even remembering their birthday are all behaviors that work to build community.

You already know people who play the community-building game. They are the ones who sent you the photocopy of a relevant article or dropped you a line to advise you of an upcoming conference. All of their efforts have created a feeling of being on the same side, in the same community, in the same territory.

You don't need to look far to find workable theories on building community and creating shared meaning. Steven Covey, author of *The Seven Habits of Highly Effective People*, calls this game "making deposits in the emotional bank account." He advises readers to make deposits of trust and cooperation in anticipation of the inevitable time when they must make a withdrawal and ask for cooperation in return. Making deposits in another's emotional bank account is an act of community building.

Community building is a proactive way to prevent territorial games. It is impossible to play territorial games and build community at the same time. Agreeing to play the community-building game edges out old territorial games from your organizational repertoire.

Any new game that serves as a countermeasure to old territorial games will help change the behavior patterns in your organization. The trick is to let the group design its own game. When a group discovers its own solution, it lasts longer. You can suggest game names, like the recruitment game, building bridges game, or community service game. One group designed the secret champion game and matched partners across departmental lines, charging them with operating as each other's liaison when internal conflicts arose. The secrecy made it fun, and the game dramatically changed the atmosphere of the two departments.

Jump-Starting Our Evolution

Evolving new games that are better adapted to our new environment is a process of evolution. The good part about being human is that we can consciously choose the direction in which we want to evolve. Personally, I think we have a better chance of surviving if we embrace the concept of interdependence. That means sharing the same territory with a much larger group than just those fifteen cubicles.

The world changes every day. We are dependent on technology that we don't understand. Specialization means we are dependent on people we don't know. Our marketplace spreads across geographical boundaries thousands of times larger than what people were accustomed to 100 years ago. Information is so prolific that we have to depend on others to help us sort it out. The old clear boundaries are gone. Instead of tangible goods, we depend on intangible information, decision-making power, and relationships to survive. More than ever before, we are completely dependent on the cooperation of others to survive. Yet we are still spending all our time keeping the people on whom we depend out of our territory.

Are we so tightly programmed to be territorial that we will choose to play territorial games instead of cooperating together to solve big problems? I hope not. The worst sort of territoriality is the individual or group that thinks they have cornered the market on what is "right" and what is "wrong." Invariably, the people I interviewed noted the correlation between the territorial game players and this position. One senior VP noted:

"They're very into who is right and who is wrong."

This is the sort of territoriality that prevents cooperation, not just on budgets or marketing plans, but on much bigger issues, like conservation of the environment. If we are going to adapt to our present environmental conditions, we had better get started. Nature favors natural selection as much as evolution. If we fail to cooperate, the people who are "right" may end up just as extinct as the ones who were "wrong."

The place to begin this evolution is in our organizations. If we can get marketing and accounting to talk to each other, it's a start.

Deescalating Territorial Games

You have an opportunity to choose an evolutionary direction here. Your organization is going to evolve into something new two years from now. It will be different whether you decide to contribute to that difference or not. People will have developed new patterns of behavior. And these patterns will fall somewhere along the scale from cooperative to territorial. Which way would you like to see it go? If you opt for more cooperative patterns, what sort of contribution are you willing to make to see that happen?

If your choice is to pursue cooperation and collaboration instead of giving in to territorial drives, you will have to start with yourself. Someone has to get the ball rolling in the right direction. Tending to your own territorial drives will allow you to educate yourself in the difficult realm of the emotional mind. You will find that influencing others is much easier when you have mastered how to influence you.

Remember that territoriality is not the enemy, only internal territorial games. You are territorial and will always be territorial to some extent. The trouble occurs when you are mindlessly territorial—when there is no identifiable threat and you *still* withhold information, shun a colleague, or cast a silent veto. Finding the optimal level of territoriality requires mindful consideration of when to be cooperative and when to be territorial.

Being Cooperative But Avoiding Exploitation

Since territoriality is a survival issue, it is wise to be conservative. If you lay your efforts and contributions wide open, cooperating in all directions, won't you be exploited? How can you expect your good faith efforts to be reciprocated? You can't.

You can hope they are reciprocated, but there are no guarantees that your actions will decrease the uncooperative effects of territorial games. When tackling territoriality in your group or organization, there are some clear guidelines to follow so that you end up expanded rather than exploited. These guidelines were derived from repeated trials of the prisoner's dilemma game described in Chapter 3 and other "conflict of interest" research paradigms. This is research-based advice. Based on observations of the development or deterioration of cooperation in real human beings, these guidelines combine good intentions with good common sense. So if you want to decrease territoriality in your organization, remember:

1. *Communication strongly influences the tendency to opt for a common goal.* Perceptions of common territory build from frequent experiences of common territory. Frequent communication is vital. Face-to-face communication is best. There is a big

advantage in being a friend rather than a stranger. Hiding behind the phrase "This is business, not personal" blinds you to
the fact that ultimately everything is personal. For most people,
work is their ticket to psychological survival and *that is* personal.
If you are a stranger to a group, then you are suspect. If you are
a friend, you have a much better chance to overcome a business
conflict through feelings of cooperation and shared territory.

2. *It is wise to move cautiously when trying to decrease territorial
games.* Initially it is best to hold back a little. In new groups
where feelings of inclusion have not yet developed, it can be
every man/woman for himself/herself. Over time you can increase the cooperative choices of others by increasing your own.
However, this should be thoughtfully introduced and gradually
developed. With experience, this process can be accelerated, but
it is always a step-by-step increase of expanded cooperation.

3. *If a peer continues to play territorial games regardless of your
efforts, call him on it.* Never willingly allow exploitation if you
can help it—and sometimes you can't. The behavior patterns of
your group reflect the results of those patterns. If one person is
allowed to play territorial games without correction, soon
enough that pattern will gain momentum and territorial games
will escalate. Behavior responds to immediate feedback,
whether that comes in the form of implied permission or correction. If you are on the receiving end of a territorial game, use the
Socratic method if you can. If you want to be more direct, do it
in private. But do something.

> *"What do I do to let people know they are overstepping my
> boundaries? I use subtle small communications in an indi-
> rect way. I just communicate that I know what's going on.
> It's just making them aware that I'm aware."*

Sometimes just talking about a game and its effects will be
enough to change the game. Most people are clueless about their
own territorial game playing. Don't assume that "they know
very well what they are doing." Discuss it.

4. *In a situation where territorial games are being played, retaliate at or* below *the level of intensity of the game player.* Retaliating
at a higher level of intensity spirals the games upward. Retaliat-

ing a notch below might begin a spiral downward. It sends a message but doesn't inflame the player's emotions. Even if your emotions tell you to slam a territorial game player, it is smarter to retaliate at a reduced level of intensity. If you don't respond, then you are just as responsible for contributing to the territorial games as he is.

5. *When two groups are locked in a territorial conflict, the introduction of an outside negotiator or facilitator can shift the perceptions (and thus behaviors) of the group in a way that an insider cannot.* Insiders are inevitably branded as having an allegiance to one side or the other. An outside facilitator can give the groups an opportunity to consider mutual benefits and provide new experiences that stress interdependence. Using a neutral third party in this way will increase cooperation in situations of conflicted interest.

6. *Never mindlessly cooperate in every instance.* When territorial drives are high, consistent cooperation only invites exploitation. While you may have aspirations for a totally cooperative utopia, you won't create it by dropping all your territorial drives and sharing all your resources. Shifting the norms of your group will require a conscious and considered demonstration of cooperation. A naïve, overoptimistic approach can be just as damaging to your credibility as not walking your talk. Use a contingency strategy to develop cooperation step by step.

Getting to the Root Cause

As you develop your strategy to deescalate territorial games, remember that you are dealing with emotion more than with reason. Don't try to address this issue at the level of the symptoms. You will only make it worse. Calling attention to territorial games without educating people in the root causes of territorial drives and emotional triggers is a bad idea. Calling people onto the carpet for playing these games without defusing the impulses driving these games only drives them to find even more covert ways of expressing their territorial urges. Focusing on the games alone drives the behaviors underground. You might even teach people a few tricks they didn't know before.

Teaching your group about the territorial games without

first discussing and dealing with the emotional urges that contribute to the games may only increase the sophistication and skill of the offenders. Declaring zero tolerance for game playing without some training could just create a group of fakers. This is not a manual for Machiavellians to study and then escalate the number of turf wars through some unfair advantage. A too-brief discussion of territorial games could turn out that way.

On the other hand, don't be afraid to raise the topic. Territorial games operate whether you discuss them or not. Awareness is your best defense. The more people who learn about territorial urges, the more who read this book, the less effective the strategies described here will become.

Find a way to talk about territorial games. Address the issues and bring them out in the open. Use this knowledge to better understand your own territorial urges and to help others understand theirs. Once you understand the way turf wars operate, you can end them. Imagine that: fewer territorial games and fewer internal turf wars—making you free to spend time on other things. Once you stop playing territorial games you can choose to play other, more productive games—like, let's make more money and have more fun. May the new games begin.

Bibliography

Ardrey, Robert. *The Territorial Imperative.* New York: Atheneum, 1966.

Bardwick, Judith M. *Danger in the Comfort Zone.* New York: AMACOM, 1995.

Culbert, Samuel A., and John J. McDonough. *The Invisible War: Pursuing Self Interests at Work.* New York: John Wiley & Sons, 1980.

Damasio, Antonio R. *Descartes' Error: Emotion, Reason, and the Human Brain.* New York: Avon Books, 1994.

De Bono, Edward. *I Am Right, You Are Wrong.* London: Penguin Books, 1991.

Egan, Gerard. *Working the Shadow Side: A Guide to Positive Behind-the-Scenes Management.* San Francisco: Jossey-Bass, 1994.

Goleman, Daniel. *Emotional Intelligence.* New York: Bantam Books, 1995.

Gray, Jeffrey A. *The Neuropsychology of Anxiety: An Enquiry Into the Functions of the Septo-Hippocampal System.* New York: Oxford University Press, 1982.

Groebel, Jo, and Robert A. Hinde, Eds. *Aggression and War: Their Biological and Social Bases.* New York: Cambridge University Press, 1989.

Kawasaki, Guy. *How to Drive Your Competition Crazy.* New York: Hyperion, 1995.

Krames, Lester, Patricia Pliner, and Thomas Alloway, Eds. *Aggression, Dominance and Individual Spacing: Volume 4, Advances in the Study of Communication and Affect.* New York: Plenum Press, 1978.

McGrath, Joseph Edward. *Groups: Interaction and Performance.* Englewood Cliffs, N.J.: Prentice-Hall, 1984.

Oncken, William III. Personal interview with author, February 19, 1997.

Sack, Robert David. *Human Territoriality: Its Theory and History.* Cambridge: Cambridge University Press, 1986.

Scheflen, Albert E. *Human Territories: How We Behave in Space-Time.* Englewood Cliffs, N.J.: Prentice-Hall, 1976.

Service, Elman R. *Primitive Social Organization: An Evolutionary Perspective.* New York: Random House, 1971.

Stewart, Ian, and Vann Joines. *TA Today: A New Introduction to Transactional Analysis.* Chapel Hill, N.C.: Lifespace Publishing, 1987.

Stewart, Thomas A. "Your Company's Most Valuable Asset: Intellectual Capital," *Fortune,* October 3, 1994, pp. 68–74.

Taylor, Ralph B. *Human Territorial Functioning.* New York: Cambridge University Press, 1988.

Young, Paul Thomas. *Emotion in Man and Animal.* Huntington, N.Y.: Robert E. Krieger Publishing Company, 1973.

Index

About the Author

Annette Simmons, M.Ed., works for Group Process Consulting in Greensboro, North Carolina. Before becoming a consultant, she worked in the advertising, automotive, and telecommunication industries, frequently coordinating projects across international boundaries. Annette designed the "Facilitating Dialogue" and "Emotional Intelligence" workshops by Group Process Consulting. Her current research investigates the need for developing new interpersonal skills required to function in nonhierarchical work teams. She welcomes feedback from the field and can be reached at

Group Process Consulting
301 S. Elm Street, Suite 203
Greensboro, NC 27401
AnnetteGPC@aol.com